THE LITTLE BOOK
OF PHILOSOPHY

André Comte-Sponville is professor of philosophy at
the Sorbonne and the author of five scholarly works
on classical philosophy. He is also the author of the
international bestseller *A Short Treatise on the Great
Virtues*, which has been translated into twenty-four
languages.

ALSO BY ANDRÉ COMTE-SPONVILLE

A Short Treatise on the Great Virtues

André Comte-Sponville

THE LITTLE BOOK OF PHILOSOPHY

TRANSLATED FROM THE FRENCH BY
Frank Wynne

VINTAGE BOOKS
London

Published by Vintage 2005

6 8 10 9 7 5

Copyright © Editions Albin Michel S.A., Paris, 2000
This translation copyright © Frank Wynne, 2004

André Comte-Sponville has asserted his right under the
Copyright, Designs and Patents Act, 1988 to be identified as
the author of this work

First published in 2000 as
Preséntations de la philosophie

First published in Great Britain in 2004 by
William Heinemann

Vintage
Random House, 20 Vauxhall Bridge Road,
London SW1V 2SA

Random House Australia (Pty) Limited
20 Alfred Street, Milsons Point, Sydney
New South Wales 2061, Australia

Random House New Zealand Limited
18 Poland Road, Glenfield,
Auckland 10, New Zealand

Random House (Pty) Limited
Isle of Houghton, Corner of Boundary Road & Carse O'Gowrie,
Houghton 2198, South Africa

Random House Publishers India Private Limited
301 World Trade Tower, Hotel Intercontinental Grand Complex,
Barakhamba Lane, New Delhi 110 001, India

The Random House Group Limited Reg. No. 954009
www.randomhouse.co.uk/vintage

A CIP catalogue record for this book
is available from the British Library

ISBN 9780099450184 (from Jan 2007)
ISBN 0099450186

Papers used by Random House are natural, recyclable
products made from wood grown in sustainable forests.
The manufacturing processes conform to the environ-
mental regulations of the country of origin

Printed and bound in Denmark by
Nørhaven Paperback A/S, Viborg

For Christian Recchia

Contents

'Hâtons-nous de rendre la philosophie populaire!'
'Let us hasten to make philosophy popular!'

Diderot

Foreword

'Philosophy: the doctrine and exercise of wisdom (not simply science)'

Kant

To philosophise is to think for oneself; but no one can truly do so without drawing on the thoughts of others, especially those of the great philosophers of the past. Philosophy is not simply an adventure; it is also a task which cannot be accomplished without effort, without reading, without tools. As often as not the first steps are off-putting and will discourage many. This is what prompted me to publish a series of notebooks: a philosophical primer in twelve slim volumes each containing some forty, often very brief, selected texts, each prefaced by a foreword of a few pages in which I tried to summarize what seemed to me to be the essential ideas . . .

These twelve forewords, revised and considerably augmented, constitute the present volume. The modest nature of the project remains unchanged: it remains a primer, let us say one among the hundreds of doors into philosophy. It leaves to the reader the task, once you have finished the book, of setting out to discover other works, as you must do sooner or later, and, if you wish, of compiling your own anthology. Twenty-five centuries of philosophy represent an inexhaustible treasure. If this little book inspires anyone to explore, if it helps someone attain some pleasure and some knowledge, it will not have been in vain.

At first I intended these books for teenagers, but I realized from the letters I received that their readership was much wider. My original intention is still evident in the examples chosen to illustrate certain points, the perspective, the tone. The style is informal – probably because I was thinking of my own children, who are teenagers, rather than of my pupils or students with whom I have never been informal . . . I did not think it necessary to change these stylistic qualities. There is no age-limit to philosophy, but teenagers, more than adults, need a guide.

What is philosophy? I have often addressed this question, and wrestle with it again in the last of these twelve chapters. Philosophy is not a science, nor is it wisdom, nor even knowledge: it is a meditation on what knowledge is available. This is why you cannot learn philosophy, according to Kant: you can only learn to philosophize. How? By philosophizing yourself: by thinking about your own thoughts, the thoughts of others, the world, society, about what experience has taught you, and what it hasn't taught you . . . Hopefully, in doing so, you will come across a work by some professional philosopher along the way. In this way you will think better, more profoundly, more deeply. You will get farther, faster. Such a philosopher, Kant added, 'should not be considered a model of judgement, but simply an opportunity to make a judgement of him, even against him'. No one can philosophize on your behalf. Of course philosophy has its specialists, its professionals, its teachers. But it is not first and foremost a speciality, nor a job, nor a university course: it is an integral part of human existence. Since we are gifted with both life and reason, it inevitably occurs to all of us to combine these faculties. Of course it is possible to think without philosophizing (in the sciences, for example), to live without philosophizing (in moments of stupidity or passion). But it is impossible, unless you philosophize, to think your life or to live your thoughts: for that is what philosophy is.

Biology will never tell a biologist how he should live, whether he should live, or even whether he should study biology. The human sciences will never tell you what humanity is worth, or what they themselves are worth. This is why we must philosophize: because we need to think about the things we know, the things we experience, the things we desire, questions which knowledge alone cannot answer or dismiss. Art? Religion? Politics? These are important subjects, but subjects which themselves must be questioned. And as soon as you begin to question them, to think about them deeply, you step outside the subjects themselves: you take a step into philosophy. No philosopher would deny that philosophy itself should be questioned. But to question philosophy is not to step outside it, but to step inside.

What path should one take? I've taken the only path I am really familiar with: that of Western philosophy. This does not mean that there are no others. To philosophize is to live by reason, which is universal. Why should philosophy be the preserve of any particular group of people? Everyone knows that there are other spiritual and speculative traditions, notably in the East. But it is impossible to deal with everything, and it would be somewhat ridiculous for me to attempt to present Eastern philosophy, which I largely know only at second hand. I do not for a moment believe that philosophy is either exclusively Greek or exclusively Western. But, like most people, I believe that there has been a great philosophical tradition in the West beginning with the Greeks, and it is towards this, through this, that I would like to guide my reader. The brevity of the pieces themselves belies the vast ambition of these preludes. In a way, it should excuse their incompleteness, which is part of the definition of a prelude.

To live by reason, I said. This indicates the path – philosophy – but could never exhaust its content.

Philosophy is a radical questioning, a search for a global or ultimate truth (and not – as in the sciences – a particular truth); it entails the development and use of concepts (even though this is also a part of other disciplines), reflexive thought (thinking about the mind and about reason: thinking about thinking), meditating on one's history and that of humanity; it is a search for the greatest possible coherence, the greatest possible rationality (it is the art of reason, if you like, but it also leads to the art of living); sometimes it creates systems, but always it extrapolates theses, arguments, theories . . . Philosophy is also – perhaps first and foremost – a critique of illusions, of prejudices, or ideologies. All philosophy is a battle. Its weapon? Reason. Its enemies? Stupidity, fanaticism, obscurantism – or the philosophy of *others*. Its allies? The sciences. Its subject? Everything, with man contained within it. Or man, but within everything. Its goal? Wisdom: happiness with truth.

In practice the subjects of philosophy are numberless: nothing which is human, nothing which is true is alien to it. This does not mean that all are of equal importance. Kant, in a famous passage of *Logic*, sums up the field of philosophy with four questions: *What can I know? What should I do? What may I hope? What is man?* '. . . the first three questions relate to the last,' he remarks. But all of them, I would add, lead to a fifth which, philosophically and humanly, is probably the most important: *How should I live?* As soon as one tries to answer this question intelligently, one begins to philosophize. And since it is impossible not to pose the question, we have to conclude that we can avoid philosophy only through stupidity or obscurantism.

Should we philosophize? As soon as the question is asked, or at least as soon as we try to answer it, we are already philosophizing. This does not mean that philosophy can be reduced to self-interrogation, let alone to self-justification. To some extent, for better or worse, we philosophize every time we think (both rationally and radically) about the world, about humanity, about happiness, about justice, about death, about God, about knowledge . . . And how could we not? Man is a philosophical animal: he can renounce philosophy only if he renounces a part of his humanity.

Therefore we must philosophize: we must think as far as we possibly can, and further than what we know. The purpose? A life that is more humane, more lucid, more serene, more rational, more happy, more free . . . What we traditionally call wisdom – happiness without illusions or lies – is it something we can attain? Probably not entirely. But this should not stop us from striving for it, nor from coming closer to it. 'Philosophy,' wrote Kant, 'is man's striving for wisdom, which is ever incomplete.' All the more reason to get started immediately. Philosophy is about thinking better in order to live better. Philosophy is the work, wisdom the repose.

What is philosophy? There are almost as many answers as there are philosophers. This does not mean that they do not agree on the essentials. Since my student days I have always had a particular fondness for Epicurus' answer: 'Philosophy is an activity, which, through discourse and reasoning, procures for us a happy life.' This defines philosophy by its greatest achievement (wisdom, bliss) and it is better to define it thus, even if the achievement is never absolute, than to confine it to its failures. Happiness is the goal; philosophy the path. *Bon voyage!*

Note on the Translation

This translation follows the French convention of using the masculine pronoun 'he' when referring to people in general; it should of course be read to include people of both sexes.

1: Ethics

'It is better to be a human being unsatisfied than a pig satisfied; better to be Socrates unsatisfied than a fool satisfied. And if the fool or the pig is of a different opinion, it is because they only know their own side of the question. The other, to make the comparison, understands both sides.'

John Stuart Mill

People have the wrong idea about ethics. It does not exist primarily to punish, to repress, to condemn. There are courts, police and prisons for that and no one would claim they are governed by pure morality. Socrates died in prison, but he died more free than his judges. It is here, perhaps, that philosophy begins. It is here that ethics begins, ceaselessly, in each of us: at the point where no punishment is possible, no sanction is effective, no condemnation – at least no external condemnation – is necessary. Ethics begins when we are free: it is freedom itself, when that freedom is considered and controlled.

In a shop, you see a CD or a jacket you'd like to steal . . . but there's a security guard watching you, or maybe there's a CCTV system, or maybe you're just scared of being caught, of being punished, of being condemned . . . This is not honesty; it is self-interest. It is not ethics; it is caution. Fear of the police is the opposite of virtue, or it is the virtue of prudence.

Imagine, on the other hand, that you had the ring that Plato wrote about, the famous *ring of Gyges*, which enables you to become invisible at will . . . It was a magical ring, discovered by a shepherd . All he had to do was turn the stone towards the palm of his hand to become completely invisible, and turn it back to become visible again . . . Gyges, who until then had appeared to be an honest man, couldn't resist the temptations offered by the ring: he used its magical powers to enter the palace, seduce the queen, assassinate the king, seize power for himself and exercise it exclusively for his benefit . . . In Plato's *Republic*, the person telling the story concludes that what distinguishes a good man from a bad man, or those who appear to be good or bad, is simply prudence and hypocrisy; in other words, it is either the inordinate significance a 'good man' attaches to other people's opinions, or his ability to conceal his wickedness . . . If both the good man and the wicked man possessed Gyges' ring, there would be nothing to distinguish them:

'both would follow the same course'. This is to suggest that ethics is merely an illusion, a lie, that it is fear dressed up as virtue. It suggests that if we only had the power to make ourselves invisible, all taboos would disappear and everyone would attempt only to satisfy their personal pleasures or serve their own interests.

Is this true? Plato, of course, thought not. But you don't have to be a Platonist . . . The only valid response, inasmuch as it concerns *you*, is within you. Imagine – this is a thought experiment – imagine that you have the ring. What would you do? What would you not do? Would you continue to respect other people's property, for example, their privacy, their secrets, their freedom, their dignity, their lives? No one can answer for you: the question concerns you alone, but it concerns you entirely. Anything that you do not do now but would permit yourself were you invisible owes less to ethics than it does to prudence or hypocrisy. On the other hand, that which you would still require of yourself or forbid yourself, even if you were invisible – not out of self-interest, but from a sense of duty – that alone is strictly moral. Your soul has its touchstone. Your morality has its touchstone by which you judge yourself. Your morality is that which you require of yourself, not because of what others might think, nor because of some external threat, but in the name of a particular conception of good and evil, of duty and of proscription, of what is acceptable and unacceptable, of humanity and of yourself. In practical terms: morality is the sum total of the rules to which you would submit, *even were you invisible and invincible.*

Is that a lot? Is it a little? That is for you to decide. If you could make yourself invisible would you condemn an innocent man, for example, or betray a friend, beat a child, would you rape, torture, murder? Only you can answer; your ethics depends entirely on your answer. Even though you don't have the ring, that doesn't prevent you from thinking, judging, acting. If there is a difference, beyond appearances, between the villain and the honest man, it is that, for the latter, what others think is not everything, prudence is not everything. This is the wager of ethics, and its ultimate solitude: all ethics connects us to others, but also connects us to ourselves. To act ethically is, obviously, to be considerate of the interests of others, but 'unobserved by either gods or men', as Plato puts it, that is to say without hope of reward or punishment, requiring no one but oneself to witness the act. Is it a wager? Maybe I've expressed myself badly, since the answer, once again, depends entirely on you. It is not a gamble, it is a choice. Only you know what you should do, no one else can make the decision for you. The solitude and power of ethics is that you are only as good as the good that you do, as the evil that you refrain from doing, all with no other reward than the satisfaction – even if no one ever knows of it – of having done good.

This is what Spinoza means by reason: 'Act well and rejoice.' This is reason itself. How can you be happy unless you have some self-respect? And how can you respect yourself unless you control yourself, master yourself, overcome your failings? The ball is in your court, as they say, but it's not a game, still less an exhibition match. This is your life: right here, right now, you *are* what you *do*. Ethically speaking, it's pointless wishing you were someone else. You can dream of being rich, healthy, good-looking, happy . . . But it is absurd to dream of being virtuous. Whether you are a villain or a good person is for you and you alone to decide: you are *worth* precisely what you *want*.

What is ethics? It is the sum total of those things that an individual imposes on himself or denies himself, not primarily to further his own welfare or happiness – that would be nothing more than egotism – but in consideration of the interests or the rights of others, in order to avoid being a villain, in order to stay true to a certain conception of humanity and of himself. Ethics is the answer to the question: 'What should I do?' It is the sum of my duties, in other words of the imperatives which I believe to be legitimate – even if from time to time, as everyone does, I break them. It is the law which I impose – or which I should impose – upon myself; independently of the judgement of others and of any expectation of reward or sanction.

'What should I do?' and not: 'What should others do?' This is what distinguishes ethics from moralizing. 'Ethics,' according to Alain, 'is never for one's neighbour': someone who is preoccupied by his neighbour's duties is not moral, but a moralizer. Is it possible to imagine a more unpleasant person, a more pointless task? Ethics is legitimate only in the first person singular. To say to someone: 'You ought to be generous' displays no generosity. To say: 'You should be brave' is not an act of bravery. Ethics is valid only for oneself; duty applies only to oneself. For others, compassion and the law are enough.

Besides, who can know another's intentions, his reasons or his merits? None can be morally judged except by God, if he exists, or by himself – and that is sufficient. Have you been selfish? Have you been cowardly? Have you taken advantage of another's weakness, his distress, his innocence? Have you lied, stolen, raped? You know all too well, and that self-knowledge is what we call conscience. From an ethical standpoint, it is the only judge that matters. A trial? A fine? A prison sentence? These are the trappings of human justice; nothing but a matter of police and lawyers. How many thugs are walking free? How many honest men in prison? You may be able to square yourself with the laws of society, and no doubt you should. But that does not exempt you from squaring yourself with yourself, with your conscience, which is in fact your only true law.

Are there then as many ethics as there are individuals? Absolutely not. This is the paradox of ethics: it applies only in the first person singular, but it also applies universally, in other words to every human being (since every human being is an 'I'). That, at least, is how we act. We know that in practice ethics may differ depending on one's education, the society and the era in which one lives, the circles in which one moves, the culture with which one identifies . . . There is no absolute ethics, or at least none that anyone can fully know. But when I abstain from cruelty, racism or murder, it is not simply a question of personal preference, something which depends on individual tastes. It is, essentially, a question of the survival of – and the dignity of – society as a whole, in other words of humanity, of civilization.

If everyone lied, no one would believe anyone any longer: in fact it would become impossible even to lie (since lying presupposes the trust which it betrays) and all communication would become absurd or futile.

If everyone stole, life in society would become impossible or miserable: there would no longer be any concept of ownership, no well-being for anyone and nothing left to steal . . .

If everyone killed, humanity and civilization themselves would be on the road to ruin: there would be nothing but violence and fear, and we would all be victims of ourselves, the killers . . .

These are only hypotheses, but they take us to the crux of what ethics is. You want to know whether an act is virtuous or reprehensible? Ask yourself what life would be like if everyone behaved as you do. When a child throws chewing-gum in the street, parents say: 'If everyone behaved like you imagine all the rubbish there'd be, wouldn't it be horrible for you and for everyone else!' Imagine – at the extreme – that everyone lies, everyone kills, everyone steals, rapes, assaults, tortures . . . How could anyone wish for such a world? How could you wish such a thing on your children? How then can you exempt yourself from what you wish for? You must therefore abstain from those things which you would condemn in others or else refrain from believing yourself to be guided by the universal, that is to say by reason and the mind. This is the crucial point: to be moral is to submit *ourselves* to a law which we believe applies, or should apply, *to all*.

This is the substance of the famous Kantian expression of the categorical imperative in *Foundations of the Metaphysics of Morals*: 'Act only on that maxim by which you can at the same time will that it should become a universal law.' It is to act as humanity might act, rather than as 'little old me', to follow one's reason rather than one's inclinations or one's self-interest. An action is good only if the principle which sustains it (the 'maxim') could apply in practice to everyone: to act morally is to act in such a manner that you would wish that everyone might submit to those same principles. This corresponds to the spirit of the Gospels, or indeed the spirit of humanity (since comparable ideas are to be found in other religions), what Rousseau refer to as the 'sublime maxim': 'Do unto others as you would have them do unto you.' It corresponds, too, though more modestly and more clearly, with the spirit of compassion, once again formulated by Rousseau, 'much less perfect, but perhaps more useful than the former: *Do good to yourself with as little possible harm to others*'. It is, at least in part, to live for others, or rather for oneself, but a self which reasons and thinks. 'Alone', says Alain, 'universally . . .' This is what ethics is.

Do we need a basis to justify this ethics? It is not necessary, nor perhaps even possible. A child is drowning. Do you need to justify your decision to save him? A tyrant massacres, oppresses, tortures . . . Do you need to justify your decision to oppose him? Such a basis could only be an incontestable truth which would guarantee the value of our values: it would enable us to prove, even to someone who does not share our values, that we are right and he is wrong. But in order to do this we would have to provide a basis for reason itself, and that is something which we cannot do. What proof is possible without a prior principle which would in turn have to be proven? In any case, what basis can there be for a morality which postulates the very morality which it sets out to prove? How can we prove to a person who prizes selfishness over generosity, lying over honesty, violence and cruelty over gentleness and compassion, that he is wrong, and what would it mean to him if we could? Why should someone who thinks only of himself care about reason? Why would someone who lives only for himself care about universal principles? Why would someone who does not hesitate to violate the freedom of others, the dignity of others, the lives of others pay the slightest attention to the principle of non-contradiction? And why, if we are to do battle with him, would we need arguments to refute him? Horror cannot be refuted. Evil cannot be refuted. In the war against violence, against cruelty, against barbarism we need courage rather than an ethical basis. And for ourselves, we need discipline and loyalty rather than an ethical basis for our actions. What is essential is to prove that we are not unworthy of what humanity has made of itself. Why should we need a basis or a safeguard for this? How could such a thing be possible? Will is sufficient, and is worth far more.

'Ethics,' writes Alain, 'consists of knowing that one is of the spirit and, therefore, is obligated absolutely; *noblesse oblige*. There is nothing more to ethics than one's sense of one's own dignity.' Ethics is a respect for one's own humanity and that of others. This does not come without self-denial, without effort, without struggle. It requires you to deny that part of you which does not think, or which thinks only of itself. It requires you to refuse – or at least rise above – your own violence, your own selfishness, your own baseness. It requires you to strive to be a man or a woman and to be worthy of it.

'If God does not exist,' one of Dostoyevsky's characters says, 'then everything is permitted.' But this is not true, since, whether or not you believe in God, you do not permit yourself everything: *everthing* – including the worst – would be unworthy of you!

A believer who respected ethics merely in the hope of heaven or the fear of hell would not be virtuous: he would simply be selfish and prudent. Someone who does good only that he may be saved, to paraphrase Kant, does no good, and will not be saved. That is to say that an action is good, ethically speaking, only on condition that it does not depend, as Kant says, 'on the result expected from that action'. It is at this point that we come to modernism, or secularism (in the most positive sense, the sense in which a believer can be as secular as an atheist). It is the spirit of the French Enlightenment philosophers. The spirit of Bayle, of Voltaire, of Kant. Religion is not the foundation of ethics; rather it is ethics which provides the foundation for – which justifies – religion. It is not because God exists that I should do good; it is because I must do good that I may need – not to feel virtuous, but to escape despair – to believe in God. It is not because God commands something that it is good; it is because a commandment is morally good that I can believe that it comes from God. Thus ethics does not preclude belief; in fact, as Kant says, it gives rise to religion. But it is not dependent upon it, nor can it be reduced merely to it. Even if God should not exist, even if there were nothing after death, that would not exempt you from doing your duty, in other words, from acting compassionately.

'Nothing is so beautiful, so right,' wrote Montaigne, 'as acting as a man should.' One's only duty is to be human (in the sense in which to be human is not merely to be a species of animal, but to act in the light of the collective knowledge of civilization), the only virtue is to be human, and this is something which no one can do on your behalf.

This does not replace happiness, which is why ethics is not everything. It does not replace love, which is why ethics is not the most important thing. But happiness does not make it any less necessary, nor is love sufficient to replace it: morality, therefore, is necessary.

It is this which enables you, while being free to be yourself (rather than remaining a prisoner of your instincts and your fears), to live freely among others.

Ethics is a universal (or at least potentially universal) necessity which has been conferred upon you *personally*.

It is by doing good to man and to woman that one helps humanity to exist. And it is necessary: it needs you just as you need it!

2: Politics

'We must think about politics, if we do not think about it sufficiently we will be cruelly punished.'

Alain

Man is a social animal: he can only grow and flourish among others of his kind.

But he is also a selfish animal. His 'unsocial sociability', as Kant calls it, means that he can neither live without others nor abandon, for their sake, the satisfaction of his own desires.

This is why we need politics. So that conflicts of interest can be resolved without violence. So that our forces can be united rather than opposed. So that we can avoid war, fear, barbarism.

We need to found a State, not because all men are good and just, but because they are not; not because they are united, but so that they may have a chance to become so. Not 'by nature', contrary to what Aristotle says, but through culture, through history. That is the definition of politics: history as it is made, unmade and remade, as it moves forward; history in the present tense; it is our history, and it is the only history. How can you not be interested in politics? You might as well not be interested in anything, since everything else depends on it.

What is politics? It is the management of conflicts, alliances and balances of power without resort to war – not simply between individuals (as in a family or some other group) but in society as a whole. It is the art of living together, within a single State or city (*polis*, in Greek) with others whom we have not chosen, to whom we feel no particular attachment and who, in many respects, are rivals rather than allies. This supposes shared power, and a struggle for that power. It supposes government, and changes of government. It supposes conflicts (albeit governed by rules), compromises (albeit provisional), and eventually agreement on how to resolve disagreements. Without politics, there would be only war and that is what it must prevent in order to exist. Politics begins where war ends.

It entails knowing who gives orders and who obeys, who *makes the law*, who or what is the sovereign. This can be a king or a despot (in an absolute monarchy), it can be the people (in a democracy), it can be a particular group of individuals (a social class, a political party, a real or presumptive elite: an aristocracy) . . . It can be, and often is, a particular mix of these three types of regime or government. Whichever is the case, politics could not exist without this power, which is the greatest of all – on this earth at least – and the guarantee of all others. For 'power is everywhere' as Foucault said, or rather, there are innumerable forms of power; but they can only coexist under the accepted or imposed authority of the strongest amongst them. A multiplicity of powers and a unity of sovereign or State power: this is the field on which politics is played out, and that is why it is necessary. Are we to submit to the first thug who comes along? To the first petty tyrant? Of course not! We know that we must submit to some power, or perhaps several, but we should not submit to just anyone, nor should we do so at any price. We wish to choose to obey: we want the authority to which we submit, far from taking away our own power, to reinforce and safeguard it. In this, we do not always quite succeed, nor do we ever quite abandon our quest. This is why we engage in politics. It is why we continue to do so. So that we can be freer. So that we can be happier. So that we can be stronger. Not individually stronger, nor pitted one against the other, but 'all together', as the protestors in the French General Strike of 1995 said; or, rather, together but opposed – since otherwise there would be no need of politics.

Politics presupposes disagreement, conflict, contradiction. When everyone agrees (that health is better than illness, happiness better than unhappiness), there is no need for politics. But neither is it politics when everyone keeps to himself, or cares only for his own affairs. Politics brings us together so we may oppose one another: it pits us against one another in the best way possible. Politics is unending. People are mistaken when they say that politics is dead: if it were, it would mean the end of humanity, the end of freedom, the end of history, all of which endure, and must endure through conflicts which are acknowledged and overcome. Politics, like the sea, endlessly renews itself. It is both a battle and the only possible peace. Let me repeat: it is the opposite of war, and that alone speaks to its greatness. It is the opposite of the natural state, and that alone speaks to its necessity. Who would wish to live alone? Who would wish to live in constant conflict with others. The natural state, as Hobbes points out, is 'where every man is enemy to every man': and man's life is therefore 'solitary, poor, nasty, brutish and short'. Much better to share power, to have a common law, to have a State: politics is better than such a life!

How do we live together, and what is our goal? These are the twin problems we struggle to solve, only to begin again immediately (since everyone has the right to change his mind, his party, his allegiance . . .) Each has a duty to reflect, to discuss.

What is politics? It is the conflicts of a life lived within society where each is governed by the State and each strives to control it: it is the art of taking, retaining and wielding power. It is also the art of sharing, if only because there is no other way to take power.

It would be wrong to think of politics as a secondary or contemptible activity. In fact, the opposite is true: to govern a community, its shared destiny, its shared conflicts, is a task which is essential to every human being, one from which no one is exempted. Are we to leave the way open to fascists and demagogues? Are we to allow bureaucrats to make our decisions for us? Are we to let technocrats or careerists mould society in their image? If so, what right do we have to complain when things go wrong? How can we pretend not to be complicit in the mediocre – or the worst – if we do nothing to prevent it? Inaction is not an excuse. Incompetence is not an excuse. To refuse to participate in politics is to surrender a part of our power, and this is always dangerous; but it is also to renounce some of our responsibilities, which is always reprehensible. To be apolitical is both mistaken and wrong: it is to go against our interests *and* our duties.

But it would be equally wrong to equate politics simply with morality, as though it were concerned only with goodness, virtue and disinterestedness. Once again, the opposite is true. If morality reigned, there would be no need of police, laws, courts, armies: we would have no need of a State and consequently no need of politics! To rely on morality to prevail over misery and injustice is simply to delude oneself. To rely on humanitarianism as a form of foreign policy, charity as a form of social policy, and anti-racism as a form of immigration policy, is to delude oneself. That is not to say that humanitarianism, charity and anti-racism are not fundamental moral qualities, but politically they are incapable of solving even the least social problem (if they were, we wouldn't need politics any more).

Morality operates across borders, politics operates within them. Morality owes no allegiance to country, politics does. It goes without saying that neither morality nor politics attributes the least importance to race: the colour of your skin does not in any way affect your humanity or your citizenship. But morality has nothing whatever to do with France or the French, Europe or Europeans. Morality refers only to the individual: only to humanity. Whereas, whether right- or left-wing, French or European, politics exists to protect the interests of a specific people or peoples – not to the exclusion of humanity – that would be immoral and suicidal – but as a priority, something which morality could neither approve nor absolutely prohibit.

We might wish morality were sufficient, humanity were sufficient: we might wish that politics were unnecessary. But to do so would be to misunderstand history and to deceive ourselves.

Politics does not stand in opposition to selfishness (as morality does), it is a collective, conflicted expression of it: it is a matter of being selfish together, and being so as effectively as possible. How? By working towards a convergence of our interests, towards something we call solidarity (as opposed to generosity, which implies disinterestedness)

The distinction between the two is often mis-understood, so I will underline the point. It is true that if I show solidarity, I am defending the interests of others, but only because – directly or indirectly – it is also in my interests to do so. In acting on someone else's behalf, I am also acting on my own, because we have common enemies, common interests, because we face common dangers. This is the principle behind trade unionism, insurance and taxation. No one would argue that having insurance, being a member of a union or paying taxes is a mark of generosity. Generosity is something very different: it consists in defending the interests of others, not because they are also mine, but despite the fact that I do not share them; not so that I can get something out of it, but so that someone else might. I am acting on someone else's behalf, but not on my own: it is possible, in fact it is likely, that I stand to lose. How can you keep what you give? How can you give what you keep? That would no longer be a gift but an exchange: not an act of generosity but one of solidarity.

Solidarity is a way of collectively defending oneself; generosity, when it comes down to it, is sacrificing one-self for others. This is why, morally speaking, generosity is superior; it is also why socially and politically speaking, solidarity is more crucial, more realistic, more effective. No one makes their social security contributions out of generosity. And it would be a rare union member indeed who joined a union purely out of generosity! Nonetheless, social security, unions and taxation have done more for social justice – much more! – than the scant generosity we occasionally display. This is true, too, of politics. No one respects the law out of generosity. No one is a citizen out of generosity. But the law and the State have done much more for justice and for freedom than fine sentiments.

This is not to say that solidarity and generosity are incompatible: being generous does not prevent one from showing solidarity; showing solidarity does not preclude one from being generous. But neither are they equivalent, and this is why neither is sufficient in itself, nor is either capable of substituting for the other. Rather, generosity might be sufficient, were we sufficiently generous. Unfortunately we are generous so inadequately and so infrequently and when we are, our generosity is so meagre . . . We need solidarity only because we lack generosity, and because we do, we badly need solidarity.

Generosity is a moral virtue, solidarity a political one. The business of the State is to regulate and socialize the demands of competing egotisms. This is why it is necessary. That is why it is irreplaceable. Politics is not a matter of morality, duty, or love . . . It is a matter of power-struggles, differences of opinion, vested interests and conflicts of interest. Look at Machiavelli or Marx. Look at Hobbes or Spinoza. Politics is not a form of altruism: it is intelligent, socialized egotism. This is not to condemn it, but to justify it: since everyone is selfish, we might as well be selfish intelligently and collectively! It is obvious that the patient, logical pooling of interests is better for almost everyone than universal confrontation and chaos. It is obvious that justice is better for almost everyone than injustice. It is obvious that such solidarity is morally justified, and demonstrates that morality and politics do not have opposing goals. But it is obvious, too, that morality is not sufficient to achieve such goals, which demonstrates that morality and politics are not to be confused.

Morality is, by definition, disinterested; not so any political system.

Morality is, or strives to be, universal; politics is always particular.

Morality is individual (it applies only in the first person singular); politics is collective.

This is why morality cannot take the place of politics, any more than politics can take the place of morality: we need both, and need the difference that exists between them!

Elections, with occasional exceptions, are not confrontations between the good guys and the bad guys: they involve opposition between different camps, different social or ideological groups, parties, alliances, vested interests, opinions, priorities, choices, political platforms . . . Of course, morality plays a part (it is possible for a vote to be morally reprehensible). But that should not distract us from the fact that morality is not a platform or a policy. What is morality's policy for tackling unemployment, war, barbarism? True, it tells us that we *should* tackle them, but does not tell us *how* to overcome them. *How* is precisely what is important in politics. Are you in favour of justice and liberty? Morally, that is a bare minimum. But politically, that does not tell you how to safeguard – or to reconcile – justice and liberty. We might believe that the Israelis and the Palestinians should each have secure, internationally recognized States; that the inhabitants of Kosovo should be able to live in peace; that globalization should not trample peoples and individuals; that every senior citizen should enjoy a decent retirement and every young person enjoy an education worthy of the name. Morality would heartily approve such sentiments, but it will not tell us how, together, we might increase the chances of achieving these things. Does anyone really believe that economics and the free market are sufficient in themselves? Markets are valid only for commodities. But our world is not a commodity, nor are justice or freedom. It would be madness to entrust to market forces things which cannot be for sale! As for companies, they are motivated primarily by profit. I am not condemning them for this: it is their function, and each of us depends on their profits. Who could possibly believe that profit alone is sufficient to ensure a humane society? The economy produces wealth; we need wealth, we can never have too much of it. But we also need justice, freedom, security, peace, fraternity, hopes, ideals . . . No market can provide these things. This is why we must engage in politics: because neither morality nor economics are sufficient in themselves and it would therefore be morally reprehensible and economically disastrous for us to muddle along.

Why politics? Because people are neither saints nor mere consumers: we are citizens; and that is how it should be. Politics makes it possible for us to continue to be citizens.

As for those who make a career in politics, we should be grateful for their efforts on behalf of the public interest; equally, we should have no illusions as to their competence or their virtue: vigilance is a human right and a citizen's duty.

Such democratic vigilance should not be confused with ridicule, which makes everything ridiculous, nor with contempt, which makes everything contemptible. To be vigilant is not to take every man at his word; neither is it to condemn or pour scorn on everything as a matter of principle. We will never succeed in rehabilitating politics – something we urgently need to do – by continually hurling abuse at those who practise politics. In a democratic state, we get the politicians we deserve. Another reason to prefer such a system over all others is that no one has the moral right to criticize it – and there are many reasons to criticize it – unless he is prepared to work together with others to change it.

It is not enough to hope for justice, peace, liberty and

prosperity . . . We must work to safeguard and to nurture them, which we can do effectively only as a collective and, consequently, through politics. I have emphasized that politics cannot be reduced simply to morality nor to economics. However, that is not to say that it is morally indifferent nor that it lacks an economic dimension. For any individual concerned with human rights and with his own well-being, being involved in politics is not simply a right: it is also his duty, and in his interests – and perhaps the only means by which those duties and interests may be reconciled. Between the law of the jungle and the laws of love there is the law itself. Between the purity of angels and the savagery of beasts, there is politics. Angels can get by without. Beasts can get by without. Mankind cannot. This is why Aristotle was right, in one sense at least, to write that 'man is a political animal' because without politics, he would be unable to fully embrace his humanity.

'Acting as a man should' (morality) is not enough. We must also fashion a society which is humane (since it is society which, in many respects, fashions man), and to do so, it must continually be remade, at least partially. The world is continually changing; a society which did not change with it would be doomed. We must therefore work, struggle, resist, invent, safeguard, reform . . . This is the purpose of politics. Are there more interesting tasks? Perhaps. But on a social scale, there are none more important. History does not stand still; it does not hang around foolishly and wait!

History is not Fate, it is not simply those things which happen to us: it is also those things we make happen, those things which shape us, and that is the very definition of politics.

3: *Love*

'To love is to rejoice'

Aristotle

Love is the most interesting of subjects. In itself, because of the happiness it promises or seems to promise – or which it takes or threatens to take away. What topic of conversation could be more pleasant between friends, more intimate, or more emotive? What word could be more secret between lovers, more tender, more troubling? And what could excite more passion between two people than passion itself?

It might be said that love is not the only passion nor passion the only form of love . . . This is true, but simply confirms my point: love is the most interesting of subjects, not only by itself – in the happiness it promises or threatens – but even indirectly, because every passion lays claim to it. What are you most passionate about?

Sport? Then you love sport! Films? Then you love the cinema! Money? Then you love money or the things it can buy you. Politics? Then you love politics, or power, or justice, or freedom . . . Your work? Then you love your work, or at least what it can offer you or will one day offer you . . . Your own happiness? Then you love yourself, as everyone does: happiness is probably no more than loving who you are, what you have and what you do . . . Are you interested in philosophy? 'Love' is part of the word itself (*philosophia*, in Greek, is the love of wisdom), and part of its meaning (what greater wisdom is there than to love?). Socrates, revered by all philosophers, did not claim otherwise. You might even be interested in fascism, in Stalinism, in war? Then you love them, or alternatively – and more justifiably – you love those things which contend with them: democracy, human rights, peace, fraternity, courage . . . There are as many different loves as there are interests. But there can be no interest without love, and this brings me back to my original point: love is the most interesting of subjects, and no other subject is of interest except inasmuch as we invest it with love or find love in it.

We must therefore love love itself, or love nothing – we must love love or die; this is why love, not suicide, is the only truly serious philosophical problem.

I am referring to the opening of Albert Camus's *The Myth of Sisyphus*: 'There is but one truly serious philosophical problem, and that is suicide. Judging whether or not life is worth living amounts to answering the fundamental question of philosophy.' I happily subscribe to the second proposition, and it is this which prevents me from wholeheartedly agreeing with the first. Is life worth living? Suicide eliminates rather than resolves the problem; only love, which does not eliminate it (since the question is posed again every morning, every evening), comes close to resolving it, for as long as we are alive, for as long as it keeps us alive. Whether life is or is not worth the pain of being lived, or, rather, whether it is worth the pain *and the pleasure* of being lived depends, first and foremost on one's capacity for love. This is what Spinoza realized: 'One's happiness or unhappiness, indeed, is made to depend entirely upon the quality of the object which one loves.' Happiness is to be happy in love, unhappiness is to be unhappy in love, or to have no love at all. Depressive psychosis or melancholy, Freud would say, is characterized primarily by 'the loss of the capacity to love' – including the ability to love oneself. It is hardly surprising, therefore, that it is so often suicidal. It is love which keeps us alive, since it alone makes life loveable. It is love which saves; it is therefore love which must be saved.

But what love? And what object of love?

For love is clearly as diverse as its objects are numberless. We may love money or power, as I have said, but we may also love our friends, our partners, our children, our parents, indeed anyone at all: someone who simply happens to be there, which is what it means to love one's neighbour.

We may love God, too, those who believe in him, and believe in ourselves if we love ourselves even a little.

Using one word to refer to so many different affections gives rise to confusion and – since desire inevitably comes into play – to illusion. Do we know what we talk about when we talk about love? Do we not often take advantage of the equivocal nature of the word to conceal or to embellish equivocal loves (by which I mean those which are selfish or narcissistic), to delude ourselves, to give the impression that we love something other than ourselves, to conceal – rather than to correct – our errors and our lapses? Love pleases everyone. While that is understandable, it should encourage us to be more vigilant. The love of truth should go hand in hand with the love of love, should enlighten it, guide it, perhaps even temper its enthusiasm. That one should love oneself is obvious: how otherwise could we be enjoined to love our neighbour *as ourselves*? But that people often love only themselves – or only for themselves – is a risk and a danger. Why otherwise are we asked to love our neighbour *also*?

There should perhaps be different words for different loves. And it is not as though words are lacking: friendship, tenderness, passion, affection, attachment, inclination, sympathy, penchant, predilection, adoration, charity, concupiscence . . . An embarrassment of riches, and one which is, indeed, embarrassing. The Greeks, perhaps because they were more lucid than we are, or more inclined to synthesis, generally confined themselves to three words to describe three different forms of love. The three Greek words for love and, in my opinion, the most illuminating in any language are: *eros, philia, agape*. I dealt with these at length in my *Short Treatise on the Great Virtues*; here I will give only a broad outline.

What is *eros*? It is the love of that which we lack, it is also passionate love. It is Platonic love: '. . . that which he has not, that which he himself is not, and that which he is in want of, these are the objects of desire and of love.' It is the love which takes, which seeks to possess, to retain. I love you: I want you. It is the simplest form of love. The most violent form of love. How can one not love what one misses. How can one love what one does not miss? This is the secret of passion (that it thrives only in absence, unhappiness, frustration); it is the secret of religion (God is that which is absolutely absent). How can such a love, without faith, be happy? One must love that which one does not have and suffer, or have that which one no longer loves (for one loves only what one does not have) and be bored . . . The sufferings of passion, the sorrows of lovers: there is no such thing as a happy love (*eros*).

But how can we be happy without love? And how can it be that, for as long as we love, we will never be happy? Plato's concept is not entirely right, nor is it appropriate to everything. We do not only love what we do not possess: sometimes we love what is not absent – what we have, what we do, what is – and we take pleasure in them, feel joy and rejoice in that joy! This is what the Greeks call *philia* – let us call it love according to Aristotle ('To love is to be joyful') – and the secret of happiness. *Philia* is to love what we do not lack, what we take pleasure in, and this brings us joy – or rather our love itself is that joy. The pleasure of coitus and of action (the love we make), the happiness of couples and of friends (the love we share): there is no such thing as an unhappy love (*philia*).

Friendship? That is how *philia* would usually be translated, but in doing so we reduce its power and its scope. Because such 'friendship' is not bounded by desire (no longer an absence but a power), nor passion (*eros* and *philia* can, and often do, mix), nor family (Aristotle uses *philia* to denote both the love of a parent for his child and the love between spouses: much as Montaigne, later, talks of *l'amitié maritale*), nor the mystifying, infinitely precious intimacy between lovers . . . It is no longer simply what Aquinas refers to as concupiscent love (loving another for one's own sake); it is a benevolent love (loving another for the other's sake) and it is the secret of happy relationships. Certainly this benevolence does not exclude sexual love: between lovers, *philia* feeds on and is illuminated by sex. How can one not rejoice in the pleasure one gives or receives? How can we not wish the person who gives us pleasure well?

This joyful benevolence, this benevolent joy, which the Greeks called *philia*, is, as I said, Aristotle's conception of love: to love is to be joyful and to wish happiness on the person one loves. But it is also Spinoza's conception of love: 'pleasure,' he writes in the *Ethics*, 'accompanied by the idea of an external cause.' To love is to *take pleasure in*. This is why there is no other pleasure but love, it is why there is no love which, in principle, is not pleasurable. Love does not require that the object of our love be absent – it is an accidental drawback when the object of our love is missing, or when bereavement strikes and tears us apart. But such absence could not hurt us if the initial happiness, even if it were merely an illusion, were not already there. We do not simply desire what is absent; love what is absent: desire is power (the power to enjoy, the power of pleasure), love is joy. This is something all lovers know when they are happy, all friends too. I love you: I am happy that you exist.

Agape is a Greek word which appears much later. Neither Plato nor Aristotle nor Epicurus would have known the word. *Eros* and *philia* were enough for them: they knew only passion or friendship, the suffering for what is absent or the joy of what is shared. But it so happens that, long after the time of these three philosophers, an insignificant Jew in a far-off Roman colony began, in his strange Semitic tongue, to say astonishing things: 'God is love . . . Love thy neighbour . . . Love thine enemy . . .' These sentences, which would probably have seemed strange in any language, appeared to be virtually untranslatable into Greek. To what form of love could they possibly refer? *Eros*? *Philia*? Either would lead to an absurdity. How could God lack anything whatever? How could he be a friend of anyone? 'There is something ridiculous,' Aristotle had said long before, 'in claiming to be God's friend.' It is pretty difficult to imagine how our lives, so insignificant, so pitiful, could add anything to His eternal, perfect divine joy . . . And who could reasonably ask us to fall in love with our neighbour (that is to say anyone and everyone!) or, absurdly, to be friends with our enemies? Still, these teachings had to be translated into Greek, as nowadays one would translate something into English so that it could be understood throughout the world . . . In order to do so, Jesus' early disciples – since obviously it is his teachings I am referring to – were obliged to devise – or popularize – a neologism created from a verb (*agapan*: to love) which as a rule had no substantive form: the word was *agape*, which was translated into Latin as *caritas*, and which in English is usually translated as *charity*. What does it mean? It means love of one's neighbour, inasmuch as it is possible: to love someone who neither saddens us by his absence, nor makes us happy by his presence (someone, in other words, who is neither a lover nor a friend), someone who exists, who merely exists, and whom we must love uselessly, for no reason, or rather purely for his sake, regardless of who he is, regardless of his worth, regardless of what he does, even if he is our enemy . . . This is Christ's conception of love, it is also that of Simone Weil or Vladimir Jankelevitch, and it is the secret of sanctity – if such a thing exists. We should not confuse this compassionate and loving *charity* with the giving of alms nor with condescension: rather it is a spirit of universal friendship, completely liberated from the *ego* (which ordinary friendships are not: 'because it was him, because it was me', as Montaigne wrote of his friendship with La Boétie), liberated from egotism, liberated from everything and therefore in itself liberating. It is the love of God, if He exists ('*O Theos agape estin*' as St John writes in his first epistle: God is love), and if God does not exist, it is that which comes closest to Him in our hearts and in our dreams.

Eros, *philia*, *agape*: love which is yearning or possessing; love which is joyful and which is shared; love which is welcoming and giving . . . Can there be happiness without longing? How can one give without sharing? If we must distinguish, at least intellectually, between these types of love, or these three degrees of love, it is chiefly so that we understand that all three are necessary and intertwined, and to illuminate the path which leads from one to another. They are not three discrete, mutually exclusive entities; they are rather three points in a single realm, the realm of love, or three possible impulses in the process we call life. *Eros* is the beginning, something of which Freud, after Plato or Schopenhauer, reminds us; *agape* is the goal (towards which we may at least strive), something which the Gospels continually tend towards; lastly, *philia* is the path, or it is joy as a path: that which transforms longing into power, poverty into riches.

Imagine a baby at the breast; his mother giving him suck. She, too, was once a child: we all begin by taking, and that too is a form of love. Later, we learn to give, at least a little, at least sometimes, to do so is the only way to be completely faithful to the love we have received; this all-too-human love, so fragile, so hesitant, so limited, a love which nonetheless gives us a glimpse of something infinite; this love of which we are the object and which has made subjects of us; this love, unearned, which preceded us, through which we were begotten not created; this love which cradled us, washed, fed, protected and consoled us; this love which is always with us, for which we long, in which we rejoice, which moves us and which illuminates us . . . If there were no mothers, what would we know of love? If there were no love, what would we know of God?

A *philosophical* declaration of love might look like this:

> There is Plato's conception of love: 'I love you, I long for you, I want you.'
>   There is Aristotle's and Spinoza's conception of love: 'I love you: you are the cause of my happiness and I rejoice in you.'
>   There is Simone Weil's or Vladimir Jankelevitch's conception of love: 'I love you as I love myself, who am nothing, or almost nothing, I love you as God loves us, if He exists, I love you as I love anyone: my strength is

here to serve your weakness, my feeble strength at the service of your great weakness . . .'

Eros, philia, agape: *the love which takes, which knows only joy or suffering, possession or loss; the love which rejoices in sharing, which wishes happiness on those who make us happy; lastly, the love which accepts and protects, which gives of itself, abandons itself, which no longer needs to be-loved . . .*

I love you in all of these ways: I take you eagerly, I joyfully share your life, your bed, your love, I give myself, abandon myself tenderly . . .

Thank you for being what you are: thank you for being, and for helping me to be!

4: *Death*

'It is possible to provide security against other ills, but as far as death is concerned, we men live in a city without walls.'

Epicurus

To the human mind, Death is something both necessary and impossible.

Necessary, since every moment in our lives is marked by it, like a shadow from another realm (if we did not die, each moment would doubtless have a different savour, be seen in a different light), it appears to us like a vanishing point for everything.

Impossible, because there is nothing in death to think about. What is it? We do not know. We cannot know. This final mystery imbues our whole lives with mystery, like a path whose destination is unknown, or rather whose destination (death) is known only too well, though we do not know what lies beyond – beyond the word, beyond the thing itself – nor even whether there is anything at all.

This mystery may be where humanity begins (it is likely that no animal has ever speculated about it); even so, it is not as though there are no possible answers. Philosophers have always provided answers to the question: 'What is death?' Such answers make up much of metaphysics. But their answers – to simplify them crudely – fall into two categories: there are those who say that death is nothing (strictly speaking, nothingness); others who assert that there is another life, or a pure, boundless continuation of this one . . . Both are ways of denying death: as nothingness, since nothingness is nothing; or as life, since death then would simply be another life. When we think about death, it melts away: the object of the thought necessarily eludes us. Death is nothing (Epicurus), or death is not death (Plato), but another life.

Between these two extremes, it is difficult to find a middle path, except – and even this is not a middle path – to acknowledge our ignorance, our uncertainty, our doubt, maybe even our indifference . . . But since, when it comes to death, ignorance is our common lot, this third position is merely admitting what is tenuous or unknowable in the first two. Besides, these two positions are less opposing views than they are contradictory propositions, presented as axiomatic against any possible third. Either death must be something, or it must be nothing. But if it is something then, to distinguish it from nothingness, it can only be another life, either darker or more luminous than this one according to one's beliefs . . . In short, the mystery of death allows only two responses, and this may be the reason that it has so powerfully influenced humanity and the nature of philosophy: there are those who take death very seriously, as a nothingness (the majority of atheists and materialist philosophers would be included in this camp) and on the other hand there are those who see it simply as a passage, a transition between two lives, maybe even as the beginning of one's true life (which is what most religions affirm, along with most spiritualists and idealists). The mystery, of course, is not diminished by either. As I said before, when we think about death, it melts away. But that fact has never stopped anyone from dying, nor given anyone any insight into what death means.

What, we might ask, is the point of pondering a question which, for us, is insoluble? The point, as Pascal realized, is that our entire lives, our every thought depend upon it: whether or not we believe that there is 'something' after death radically influences how we live and think. In any case, if we are to interest ourselves purely in problems which can be solved (and therefore cease to be problems), we should give up philosophy. And yet how could we, unless we amputate our whole self, or at least a major part of our thought processes? Science has not provided answers to the crucial questions we ask ourselves. Why is there something rather than nothing? Is life worth living? What is goodness? What is evil? Are we free or are our actions determined? Does God exist? Is there life after death? These questions, which we might call metaphysical in the broadest sense (for they go beyond any possible physical reality), make us beings capable of thought, or rather capable of philosophizing (for the sciences also think, but do not consider these questions), and this is what makes us human or, as the Greeks would put it, *mortal*: by which they mean not those who will die – animals die too – but those who know that they will die, without knowing what that might mean and yet being unable not to think about it . . . Man is a metaphysical animal; this is why death is his constant problem. We do not need to resolve the problem, but to confront it.

'To philosophize is to learn how to die' (*'Que philosopher, c'est apprendre à mourir'*). In this form, this famous phrase is the title of one of Montaigne's *Essays* (volume I, number 20). But Montaigne expressly borrows the thought from Cicero, who attributes it to Plato in the *Tusculanes* . . . Let us say that it is Plato's idea, translated into Latin by Cicero, and into French by Montaigne . . . It doesn't matter where it comes from: what matters is that, as Montaigne pointed out, the phrase can be interpreted in two different ways. In choosing between them our whole lives – and a sizeable part of philosophy – are determined.

There is the Platonic interpretation: death, that is to say the separation of the soul from the body, is the *purpose* of life, towards which philosophy provides a sort of shortcut. Through suicide? No, on the contrary, through a life that is more spirited, more pure, more free since it is freed sooner from this prison – from this tomb, as Plato says in the *Gorgias* – which is the body . . . 'True philosophers are already dead,' writes Plato, and that is why death does not frighten them: what can it take from them?

Then there is Montaigne's interpretation: death is not 'the end' (*le but*) but 'the ending' (*le bout*) of life: its term, its culmination (not its goal). We must prepare for it, we must accept it – since one cannot escape it – without allowing it to ruin our lives or our happiness. In the early *Essays*, Montaigne attempts to think about death constantly, to become accustomed to it, to prepare for it, to steel himself – as he puts it – against it. In the later essays, the habit has become so ingrained that the thought itself seems less necessary, less constant, less urgent: acceptance is enough and, in time, that too becomes quieter, less insistent . . . This is less a paradox than it is an evolution, which marks Montaigne's achievement, or at least his progress. Anxiousness? It passes. Courage? It passes. Much better to be non-chalant, which is neither distraction nor forgetfulness, but serene acceptance. Montaigne sums this up in a single sentence, one of the most beautiful he ever wrote: 'I want us to be doing things, prolonging life's duties as much as we can; I want death to find me planting my cabbages, neither worrying about it nor the unfinished gardening.' To philosophize is to learn how to die, simply because it is to learn how to live and because death – the idea of death, the inevitability of death – is part of living. But life is what is precious. True philosophers have learned to love life as it is; why should they be frightened to be mortal?

Nothingness or rebirth? Another life, or no life? Each of us must choose between these two paths, we can even – like the sceptics, like Montaigne himself, perhaps – refuse to choose: to leave the question open, as in truth it is, and live in that *opening* that is life. But this, too, is a way of reflecting on death, and that is as it should be. For how could one not think about that which is – for all thought, for all life – the ultimate horizon?

Spinoza, by contrast, writes: 'A free man thinks of nothing less than he thinks of death, and his wisdom is a meditation not on death, but on life.' The second part of this sentence seems as obvious as the first seems para-doxical. How can one meditate on life – that is to say philosophize – without meditating, too, on its brevity, its precariousness, its fragility? I accept that the wise man (he alone is free, according to Spinoza) thinks more of being than of non-being, of life rather than of death, of his strengths rather than his weaknesses. But how can one reflect truthfully on life without thinking too – every affirmation has a negation – about its end or its mortality?

In fact, later on, in his *Ethics*, Spinoza revises what is over-unilateral in this thought. For any complete being, he explains, there is another, stronger being that can destroy him. This acknowledges that every living being is mortal, and that no one can live or persist in his being without resisting death, which threatens and assails him from every quarter. The universe is stronger than we are. Nature is stronger than we are. This is why we die. To live is to struggle, resist, survive, and no one can do so indefinitely. In the end, we must die, and it is the only end we can be certain of. To think about death constantly would be to think too much about it. But never to think about it would be to give up thinking.

Besides, no one is completely free, no one is supremely wise. This leaves thoughts of death to happy days or gruelling nights, which we must accept.

We would like there to be life after death, because that alone would allow us to definitively answer the question. But curiosity is no more an argument than hope.

In death, some see a salvation which they may attain, or in Plato's words that 'deserves to be hazarded'. Others, who expect nothing but nothingness, see death nonetheless as a respite, an end to tiredness. Both ideas are, or can be, comforting. This is one of the uses of death: to make life more acceptable either through hopefulness, or through its uniqueness. A reason, in either case, not to waste a moment of it.

I am among those to whom nothingness seems more

plausible – so plausible, in fact, that it seems a near certainty. I make the best I can of it, and all in all I do pretty well. The death of the people I love worries me less than their suffering. My own death, less than theirs. Perhaps it is something that comes with age, or with being a parent. My death will take only me; which is why when it comes I will lose everything and nothing, since there will no longer be anyone left behind to feel the loss. The death of others is real, tangible and painful in a different way. Even so, it is something each of us must face. It is what we call mourning, something which, as Freud has shown, is first and foremost something we work through ourselves, something which takes time, something without which none of us would be able to reconcile ourselves to existence. In his *Essays on Psychoanalysis*, Freud wrote: 'We recall the old saying: *Si vis pacem, para bellum.*' If you want to preserve peace, arm for war. It would be in keeping with the times to alter it: *Si vis vitam, para mortem.* If you want to endure life, prepare yourself for death. Endure? We should demand more than that. I would be more inclined to say, if you want to love life, if you want to appreciate it lucidly, do not forget that death is a part of it. To accept death – one's own, and that of those close to you – is the only way to be truthful to your life.

We are mortals and lovers of mortals, that is why we suffer. But our suffering, which makes men and women of us, is also what makes life so precious. If we did not die, if our existence did not unravel in the endless darkness of death, would life be quite so precious, so extraordinary, so moving? 'To be inconstant in your contemplation of death,' wrote Gide, 'is to devalue the smallest moment in your life.' Therefore we must think about death the better to love life – or to love it as it is: fragile and transitory – the better to appreciate it, the better to live it and, for this chapter, that is justification enough.

5: *Knowledge*

'The nature of phenomena cannot be understood by
the eyes'.

Lucretius

To know is to think what is: knowledge is a certain
relationship – of conformity, of resemblance, of sufficient – between the mind and the world, between
subject and object. This is how we know our friends, our
neighbourhoods, our houses: what is in our minds when
we think of these things corresponds more or less to what
exists in reality.

That *more or less* is what distinguishes knowledge from
absolute truth. Because we could be mistaken about our
friends. We cannot know everything about our neighbourhood. Even in our own homes, there are many things
we may be unaware of. Is it infested with termites, built
over buried treasure? There is no such thing as absolute

knowledge, infinite knowledge. Do we know our neighbourhood? Of course we do! But to know it absolutely, we would have to be able to describe every little street, every building on every street, every apartment in every building, every nook and cranny in every apartment, every speck of dust in every nook and cranny, every atom in every speck . . . How could we possibly do this? It would require perfect knowledge and infinite intelligence: neither of which is possible.

This, however, does not mean that we know nothing. If that were the case, how would we know what knowledge is, what ignorance is? Both Montaigne's question, which is one of substance ('What do I know?'), or Kant's, which is one of capability ('What can I know, how, and in what circumstances?') postulate the idea that truth is at least attainable. If it were not, how could we reason, and what would be the use of philosophy?

Reality is that which is (*veritas essendi*: the reality of existence) or that which corresponds exactly to that which is (*veritas cognoscendi*: the reality of knowledge). This is why knowledge itself cannot be absolute truth: because we can never absolutely know what is, nor all that is. We can know anything only through our senses, our reason, our concepts. How could there be such a thing as unmediated knowledge, when knowledge is, by its very nature, mediation? Our slightest thought bears the imprint of our bodies, of our minds, of our culture.

Every idea we have is human, subjective, limited, and therefore could never correspond absolutely with the inexhaustible complexity of the real.

According to Montaigne, 'Human eyes can only perceive things in accordance with such Forms as they know', and we can only think them, Kant showed, through the categories of understanding. Other eyes would show us a different landscape. Another mind would think things differently. A different brain might devise a different mathematics, a different physics, a different biology . . . How can we know things as they are *in themselves*, since to know a thing is always to perceive it, or to think of it as it appears *to us*? We have no direct access to the real (we can know it only through the medium of our senses, our reason, our instruments of observation and of measurement, our concepts, our ideas . . .), no absolute contact with the absolute, no infinite perspective of the infinite. How could we know these things completely? We are separated from the real by the very means we use to perceive and understand it; how could we know it absolutely? We can know only about specific themes. How could any themes, however scientific, be perfectly objective?

Knowledge and reality are, therefore, two very different concepts. But they also stand together. No knowledge is truth; but knowledge which contains no truth would no longer be knowledge (it would be madness, error, illusion . . .). No knowledge is absolute; but it is knowledge – rather than belief or opinion – only because of that part of the absolute it contains or makes possible.

Take the orbit of the earth around the sun, for example. No one can know it absolutely, totally, perfectly. Still, we know that it does move, and that it moves in an orbit. The theories of Copernicus and Newton, however relative they may be (since they are theories), are more true and more certain – therefore more absolute – than those of Hipparchus or Ptolemy. Similarly, the Theory of Relativity is more absolute (and not, as its name might suggest, more relative!) than the celestial mechanics of the eighteenth century, which it encompasses, but which cannot encompass it. The fact that all knowledge is relative does not mean that all knowledge is of equal value. The progress from Newton to Einstein is as indisputable as that from Ptolemy to Newton.

This is why there is a history of the sciences, and why that history is both normative and irreversible: because it opposes the more true against the less true, because we do not fall back into errors we have understood and refuted. This is what both Bachelard and Popper, after their own fashion, demonstrate. No science is definitive. But if the history of the sciences is, as Bachelard says, 'the most irreversible of all histories', it is because here progress is proven and provable: it is in fact 'the very dynamic of scientific cultures'. No theory is absolutely true, nor even absolutely verifiable. But it should be possible, in the case of a scientific theory, to verify it through experimentation, to test it, otherwise, as Popper says, to *falsify* it – in other words, to expose it as false if indeed it is. Those theories which withstand such tests replace those which fail, which they encompass or improve on. It amounts to a natural selection of theories (in Darwin's sense of the natural selection of species), through which science moves forward – not from certainty to certainty, as is sometimes believed, but through 'greater understanding and deletions' as Jean Cavaillès says; in Popper's terms 'conjectures and refutations'. In this sense scientific theories are always partial, provisional, relative, though this does not give us the right to reject them, or to favour instead ignorance or superstition – which would be to reject knowledge itself. The progress of the sciences is so great, so irrefutable, that it confirms both the relative nature of its theories (an absolute science could not progress) and their truth, however limited (a science which contained no part of truth could not progress, and would not be a science).

We should, however, be careful not to confuse *knowledge* and *science*, nor to reduce one to the other. We know a thousand and one things – address, date of birth, neighbours, friends, tastes – which science has not taught us and which it cannot prove. Perception itself is knowledge, experience is knowledge, however vague (what Spinoza refers to as knowledge of the first kind) without which all sciences would be impossible. 'Scientific truth' is therefore not a tautology: there are truths which are not scientific, and there are scientific theories which we will one day discover are not true.

Someone who is asked to testify in a court case is not asked to prove this or that fact scientifically, but simply to state what he believes or, better still, what he knows. Could he be mistaken? Of course. This is why it is always better to have several witnesses. But having several witnesses makes sense only if we postulate the possible existence of truth, without which there could be no justice. If we had no access to truth, or if truth simply did not exist, what difference would there then be between the guilty and the innocent? Between testimony and perjury? Between justice and the miscarriage of justice? And if there were no truth, then how would we fight revisionists, obscurantists and liars?

The key is not to confuse scepticism with sophistry. To be a sceptic, as Montaigne and Hume were, is to believe that nothing is certain – and we have excellent reasons to believe that that is so. We say something is certain if we are unable to doubt it. But how does one prove an inability? For centuries, men were certain that the earth was stationary: that did not stop it from turning . . . Certainty would be knowledge which has been proven. But our proofs are trustworthy only inasmuch as our reasoning is; but how can we prove our reasoning is trustworthy, since we can do so only by using our reason? 'We register the appearance of objects,' wrote Montaigne, 'to judge them we need an instrument of judgement; to test the veracity of that instrument we need practical proof; to test that proof we need an instrument. We are going round in circles.' This is the circle of knowledge, which prevents it from claiming to be absolute. How do we break the circle? We can do so only through reason or experience; but neither will suffice: experience, because it relies upon the senses; reason because it relies upon itself. 'The senses themselves being full of uncertainty cannot decide the issue of our dispute,' Montaigne goes on, 'It will have to be Reason, then. But no Reason can be established except by another Reason. We retreat into infinity.' We have a choice, therefore, between knowledge's vicious circle or an infinite series of backward steps: the result is a catch-22. The very things which make knowledge possible (the senses, reason, judgement) make it impossible for us to establish it as truth.

Jules Lequier has a striking maxim: 'When we believe with every fibre of our being that we have reached the truth, we must know that we believe, and not believe that we know.' Long Live Hume, long live tolerance!

Marcel Conche also has something striking to say about Montaigne. Doubtless we have certainties, many of which seem to be ours by right (certainties which are absolutely legitimate or justified); but 'the certainty that there are certainties by right is no more than a certainty of fact'. So we must conclude that the most unshakeable certainties, strictly speaking, prove nothing: no proofs are *absolutely* conclusive.

Should we therefore give up thinking? Absolutely not. 'It is possible that there are true proofs,' Pascal remarks, 'but it is not certain.' It cannot, in effect, be proven –

since every proof presupposes it. The proposition 'There are true proofs' cannot be proven. The proposition 'Mathematics reveals objective reality cannot be demonstrated mathematically. The proposition 'The experimental sciences reveal objective reality' cannot be proven by experiment. But this doesn't stop us from pursuing mathematics, physics or biology, nor from believing that a proof or an experiment is more valuable than an opinion. The fact that everything is uncertain is no reason to give up the search for truth, since it is also uncertain that everything is uncertain, as Pascal went on to note, and it is this fact which means the sceptics are right, even though they are unable to prove it. Long live scepticism and Montaigne! Scepticism is not antithetical to reason; it is a form of lucid rationalism taken to its logical conclusion – to that point at which reason, by virtue of its own rigorousness, comes to doubt its own apparent certainties. After all, what proof is there in appearances?

Sophism is a very different thing: it is not the belief that nothing is certain, but the belief that nothing is true. This is something neither Hume nor Montaigne ever suggested. Why, if they believed it to be true, would they have engaged in philosophy, and to what end? If scepticism is the antithesis of dogmatism, sophistry is the antithesis of rationalism. If nothing is true, what role is there for reason? How could we discuss, argue, know? We cannot say of knowledge: 'To each his own.' If we did so, there would be no truth at all, since it can be truth only if it is universal. For example, you may be the only person in the world who knows that you are reading this book. Nonetheless, it is universally true: no one, regardless of where or when he lived, could deny it without proving himself ignorant or a liar. This is why 'the universal is the domain of thoughts' as Alain remarked; it is this which makes us all equal before the truth. Truth does not do as it is told: that is why it is free, that is why it frees us.

Of course, it is impossible to prove that the sophists are wrong (since every proof postulates the existence at least of the idea of truth); but the possibility that they might be right is something which we cannot even formulate coherently. If there were no such thing as truth, the fact that there is no such thing as truth would itself be untrue. If everything were false, as Nietzsche wished, it would be false that everything was false. In this, sophistry, unlike scepticism, is paradoxical and as a philosophy self-destructs. True sophists, however, do not worry about such things. What does contradiction matter? What does philosophy matter? But philosophers since Socrates have believed that such things matter; they have their reasons, which are reason itself and the love of truth. If nothing is true, it is possible to think anything, which is convenient for the sophists; but thought is no longer possible, which is fatal to philosophy.

What I call sophism is any form of thought which defers to anything other than what appears to be the truth, or which forces truth to submit to anything other than itself (to power, to vested interest, to desire, to ideology . . .). In theory, knowledge is what keeps us from this, in practice, honesty. For if nothing were either true or false, there would be no difference between knowledge and ignorance, nor between honesty and dishonesty. Science, morality and democracy could not exist. If everything is false, everything is permitted: falsifying experiments and proofs (since none are genuine), pitting superstition against science (since there would be no truth to distinguish between them), convicting the innocent (since there would be no significant difference between true and false testimony), denying the most established truths of history (since they are as false as any other), allowing criminals to go free (since it is untrue that they are guilty), allowing oneself to indulge in criminality (because even the guilty are no longer guilty), refusing to accept the validity of any election (since an election is valid only if one can *truly* know the result) . . . The dangers are obvious. If it is possible to think anything, it is possible to do anything: sophistry leads to nihilism, as nihilism leads to barbarism.

It is this which gives knowledge its spiritual and civilizing dimension 'What is enlightenment?' asks Kant. It is man emerging from his own minority, he replies, and one can emerge only through knowledge: '*Sapere aude!*' Dare to know! 'Have the courage to make use of your own understanding!' is thus the motto of enlightenment. Without moralizing (to know is not to judge, to judge is not to know), all knowledge teaches us morality: since without it, or in opposition to it, no morality is possible.

This is why we must seek the truth, as Plato said, 'with all one's soul' – all the more so because the soul may well be nothing more than this search.

It is also why the search never ends. Not because we can know nothing, which seems highly improbable, but because it is impossible ever to know everything. The great Aristotle, with his customary flair, said it best: 'The search for truth is both difficult and easy: none can ever know it absolutely, nor miss it altogether.'

This is what allows us to go on learning and what proves the dogmatists (who claim to have the whole truth) and the sophists (who claim there is no truth, or that it is completely beyond our reach) wrong.

Between absolute ignorance and absolute wisdom, there is a place for knowledge and for progress. We simply need to work at it!

6: *Freedom*

'Obedience to a law which one prescibes to oneself is
freedom.'

Rousseau

To be free is to do as one wishes. But this can be
construed in many different ways.

Firstly, it is the freedom to *do*: freedom of action, and
as such the antithesis of constraint, of hindrance and
of slavery. Liberty, wrote Hobbes, 'is the absence of
external impediments which prevented a course of
action: as such, water held in a vase is not free, since the
vase prevents it from flowing; when the vase breaks, the
water is free again; in this sense a person enjoys liberty
proportionate to the space he is allowed.' I am free to act,
in this sense, when nothing and no one prevents me.
Such freedom is never absolute (there are always
obstacles) and rarely entirely absent. Even the prisoner

in his cell can usually choose to sit, to stand, to speak or to be silent, to plan his escape or curry favour with his gaolers . . . And no citizen in any possible State could do everything he might wish: people and laws impose certain constraints which he could flout only at his own risk. This is why such freedom is often referred to as *freedom in the political sense*: since the State is the principal agent which curtails freedom, and probably the only one which can safeguard it. Such freedom is greater in a liberal democracy than it is in a totalitarian state. And greater too in a state governed by laws than in the natural world: because only the law gives freedoms to all allowing individuals to live together rather than oppose one another, to be stronger (even if this entails mutual restrictions) rather than to destroy one another. 'Where there is no law,' Locke observed, 'there can be no freedom. For to be free means to be free from the persecution and the violence of others: something which would be impossible if there were no law.' Does the State curtail your freedom? Probably; but it also curtails the freedom of others, which is the only thing which makes your freedom real. Without laws, there would be nothing but violence and fear. Can there be anyone less free than someone who is constantly terrified or threatened?

To be free, therefore, is to *do* what we want: freedom of action, freedom in the political sense, relative physical freedom. It is the freedom of Hobbes, Locke and Voltaire ('liberty is simply the power to act'), and perhaps the only kind of freedom whose reality and whose price are incontestable.

But are we also free to *choose* what we want? This is the second sense of the word freedom: freedom to choose, freedom in the metaphysical sense, some might claim absolute freedom, even perhaps supernatural freedom. Philosophically, this is the most problematic – and the most interesting – interpretation of the word.

Let us take an example. In any democracy worthy of the name, you are free to vote for any candidate in an election. Your freedom of action in the privacy of the polling booth is total, even absolute (though it is circumscribed by the list of candidates), and therefore you can, in effect, vote for whomever you wish. Political freedom: freedom of action.

But are you also free to *choose* to vote for this candidate or that? If you are left-wing, are you *free* to choose to vote for the right? If you are right-wing, are you free to favour the left? If you fall into neither camp are you free to choose one? Can you freely choose your opinions, desires, fears and hopes? And if so, how? You could do so based on other opinions, other desires, other fears, other hopes – or you might make a purely random choice, which would immediately cease to be random. To vote *at random* would not be to vote freely. But in voting for *whom one chooses* are we not prisoner of our choices or the causes (social, intellectual, ideological . . .) which determine those choices? We make a choice based on our opinions. But who can choose his opinions?

'Human beings think themselves to be free,' wrote Spinoza, 'Insofar as they are conscious of their volitions and of their appetite, and do not even dream of the causes by which they are led to appetition and to will.' Are we free to do what we want? Of course we are! But why do we want what we want? Our choice is a part of reality: it is subjected, as everything is, to the principle of sufficient reason (nothing exists without reason: everything can be explained), the principle of causality (nothing is born of nothing: everything has a cause), and lastly to the determinism which affects macroscopic objects. And even if, at a microscopic level, there were some ultimate indeterminism (as the Epicureans believed and as quantum physics seems to confirm today), you would nonetheless be determined, at a neurobiological level, by the atoms of which you are made up. If their movements are unpredictable, they cannot then be subject to your will: it is your will, rather, which is subject to them. Randomness is not free. How could a will working at random be free?

There is a more puzzling secret than that of the polling booth: it is that which is contained within your brain, a place where no one can venture, not even you. Whose name will be ticked on the form you put into the ballot box? Are you free to choose? Certainly. But what do you know of the neural mechanism which makes that choice?

Lastly, your choice, even if we admit that you make it freely, remains subject to who you are. Millions of others will elect to vote differently. When, then, did you decide to be 'you', rather than someone else?

This is undoubtedly the thorniest part of the problem. If I do not choose who it is who chooses ('me'), all of my choices are determined by who I am, something which I did not choose, and they cannot therefore be free. But how could I possibly choose who I am, since any choice I make depends on it, and since I cannot choose anything at all unless I am already someone who has chosen to be someone or something?

This accords with Diderot's two questions in *Jacques the Fatalist*: 'Is it possible for me not to be me? And, being me, can I wish to be other?' If I cannot be other than 'me' then 'me' is a prison: how can I be free?

One should not be too hasty in concluding that such freedom does not exist, or that it is purely an illusion. To be free, as I said, is to do as one wants. To be free to choose, is to *want what one wants*. I can guarantee that this is a freedom which will never let you down; how can you not want what you want, or want something else in its place?

Far from being non-existent, the freedom to choose is, rather, something of an oxymoron: all choices are free, as the Stoics say, and it is in this sense that 'free, spontaneous and voluntary' (as Descartes describes an action in the process of taking place) are synonyms. This freedom, whose existence is not disputed by most philosophers, is what we might call the *spontaneity of desire*. This is freedom according to Epicurus and Epictetus, but also, broadly speaking, according to Aristotle, Leibniz or Bergson. It is the freedom to choose, or rather, it is choice itself when it depends solely on me (even though that 'me' is determined): I am free to desire what I desire, and that, in fact, is why I am 'me.'

Does my brain dictate my choice? Of course. But I *am* my brain, so I am dictating to myself. That I am determined by what I am proves that my freedom is not absolute, but not that it does not exist: in this sense freedom is simply the determined ability to determine my own actions. The brain, according to contemporary neuro-biologists, is an 'open self-regulating system'. Clearly I am dependent on it. But to be determined by what one is (and not some external force) is the very definition of independence! It is proper to speak of choice being *determined* to indicate that it is neither submissive nor weak. That is not the converse of freedom, it is freedom in action.

Besides, it doesn't matter whether we are talking about the brain or about an insubstantial soul. To be free, in either case, is still determined by what one is, and, in principle, on that alone. 'We are free,' Bergson writes, 'when our actions proceed from our whole personality, when they express it, when they bear that indefinable stamp that one sometimes finds which links an artist and his work.' Obviously, Raphael cannot choose to be Raphael or Michelangelo. But far from preventing him from painting freely, it is this which empowers him. How could nothingness be free? How could an impersonal being choose? 'It will be alleged, therefore, that we yield to the all-powerful influence of our character,' Bergson continues, but immediately observes that this objection is meaningless: 'Our character, too, is us,' and to be influenced by oneself (how could one not be?) is precisely what it is to be free. 'In a word,' Bergson concludes, 'if we agree that freedom is every action which proceeds from the self and it alone, then that action which bears the imprint of our personality is truly free, since only that self would lay claim to it.' This is what I mean by the spontaneity of choice. That it is determined does not in any way prevent it from determining: in fact it can determine only *because* it is determined. I don't want just anything, I want what I want, and it is in this sense that I have the freedom to choose.

Very well. But am I free to want *something other* than what I want? Is my choice a *spontaneous* freedom to choose (in other words, subject only to what I am), or an undetermined freedom to choose (which is not subject to anything, not even to what I am)? A relative freedom (if it is dependent on the self) or an absolute one (if even the self depends upon it)? Am I free to vote for the right only if I am right-wing, for example, for the left if I am left-wing, or am I in fact free to vote for *either* right or left, which would imply – except in very particular circumstances – that I am free to choose whether *to be* right- or left-wing? This secondary freedom to choose, which is mysterious (since it appears to violate the principle of identity: it postulates that I can want something other than what I want), is what philosophers often refer to as the *philosophy of indifference*, or, more usually, as *free will*. Marcel Conche gives a perfect definition of it: 'Free will,' he writes, 'is the freedom to determine oneself, undetermined by anything else.' This is freedom according to Descartes, Kant and Sartre. It postulates that what I *do* (my existence) is not determined by what I *am*, but on the contrary creates the self, or chooses it *freely*. 'What Descartes understood perfectly,' writes Sartre, 'is that the concept of freedom necessarily contains an absolute autonomy, a free act is absolutely new, no seed of which could be contained in the world as it previously was and that action and creation are therefore one.' Such freedom is only possible, as Sartre realized, if 'existence precedes essence': if man is free it is only because 'man is nothing else,' as Sartre puts it, 'but what he makes of himself'. I am free only on the condition, which I grant is paradoxical, that I choose myself absolutely: 'Every person,' Sartre writes in *Being and Nothingness*, 'is an absolute choice of self.'

This choosing of the self by the self, without which free will is impossible, unthinkable, is illustrated by Plato at the close of *The Republic* by the myth of Er (in which souls between two incarnations choose their bodies and their lives); it is what Kant called intelligible character, and it is what Sartre, in a further paradox, refers to as original freedom, which precedes all choices and upon which all choices are dependent. Such freedom is either absolute or not at all. It is the undetermined freedom to determine oneself, in other words, the power to freely create oneself. It is something which is the prerogative of God, according to some, or which makes gods of us, if indeed we have that freedom.

There are therefore two principal meanings of freedom – freedom of action and freedom to choose – the second of which subdivides in turn into two: the spontaneity of choice and free will.

Is that all? Absolutely not. Since thought is also an action: to do as one wishes can also mean to *think* what one wishes. This poses the problem of freedom of thought, or as it is referred to, independence of mind.

The problem in part retraces that of freedom of action, and therefore of freedom in the political sense. Freedom of thought (and all that it presupposes: freedom of information, of expression, of debate . . .) is a fundamental human right and an integral part of democracy.

But it goes beyond this. For example, if we imagine a mathematical problem, in what sense am I *free* to solve it? In the sense of freedom to choose? Clearly not: if I understand the proof, the solution is obvious to me, just as it escapes me if am unable to understand it. This despite the fact that no outside force constrains my thought or hinders me: I think what I wish, that is to say what I know (or believe) to be true. Without that knowledge, no freedom could be effective. If the mind had no access, however incomplete, to the truth, it would remain a prisoner of itself: its reasoning would simply be a form of madness of which every thought was merely a symptom. It is reason which frees us from this. It frees us from ourselves and opens us up to the universal. 'The mind owes no obedience,' writes Alain. 'A geometric proof is sufficient to prove this; for if you blindly accept it, you are a fool; you are betraying the mind.' This is why tyrants have no love of truth. Because truth obeys only itself: truth is free. Not because we can think whatever we like, but because the necessity of truth is the very definition of its independence.

In Euclidean space, what is the sum of the angles of a triangle? Regardless of my body, my country, my subconscious, of anything at all, I can only answer – assuming I have understood the proof – '180 degrees'. Nonetheless, it is possible that I am never more free than when, as now, I submit only to the truth as far as I know it, let us say when I submit to reason, in other words to that need in me which is not me, but which moves through me and which I understand.

There are numerous examples we could take. What is 3×7? What is the ratio of matter and energy? Who killed Henry IV? Does the sun move around the earth, or the earth around the sun? Only someone ignorant of these things can choose his answer; only someone who knows can answer freely.

Freedom of thought: freedom to reason. This is not a free choice, it is the freedom of necessity. It is the freedom of truth, or truth as freedom. This is freedom according to Spinoza, to Hegel and no doubt according to Marx and Freud: freedom as an understood necessity, or rather as an understanding of necessity.

To be free, in the true sense of the word, is to be subject only to one's own necessity, explains Spinoza: this is why reason is free, and why it frees us.

Freedom of action, spontaneity of choice, free will, freedom of thought or of reason . . . of these four meanings, each may choose the one (or more than one – they are not mutually exclusive) which seems most important or most firmly established to him. Is this choice, too, free? There can be no absolute answer, since no knowledge would be sufficient, since any answer would presuppose and depend upon a choice already made. Freedom is a mystery, at least insofar as it is a philosophical problem: we can never prove its existence, nor can we understand it completely. This mystery is what constitutes us; in this sense each of us is a mystery even to ourselves. If I have chosen to be what I am, the resulting deliberated choice could only have been made in another life – as Plato suggests – in another world – as Kant would say – or at least in another level of this world – in Sartre's terms. But of this other life, this other world, this other level, I can, by definition, have no knowledge: this is why I may believe that I am free (in the sense of having free will) without ever being able to prove it.

It is possible that this is not the most important sense of the word. Of the four possible meanings, at least three are difficult to dispute: freedom of action, spontaneity of choice, the free necessity of reason. These three freedoms have in common the fact that for us, they exist only in relative terms (we are *more or less* free to act, to choose, to know), and that is enough to establish what is at stake: the point is not whether you are completely free but rather how you can *become* more free. Free will, which is a mystery, is less important than *freeing onself*, which is a process, a goal and a task.

One is not born free, one becomes free. That, at least, is what I believe, and this freedom is never absolute, never infinite, never definitive: we are *more or less* free and our purpose, clearly, is to become as free as we are able.

It is possible that Sartre is right, but that in itself would not be sufficient to refute my last point. Whether or not we are already free does not exempt us, as Nietzsche would say, from becoming what we are. Even if each person is, as Sartre maintains, 'a self-determined self', this would not exempt us from acting, nor from choosing nor from acquiring knowledge.

Freedom is not only a mystery; it is also a goal and an ideal. Although we can never completely shed light on the mystery, this does not mean that the ideal does not enlighten us. Though the goal is unattainable, this does not prevent us from striving for it, nor from moving towards it

It is a question of learning, and of freeing ourselves: freedom is but another name, as we can see in Spinoza, for wisdom.

7: *God*

'To believe in God is to realize that life has a meaning'

Ludwig Wittgenstein

We do not know whether God exists. This is why we must question whether or not we believe.

'. . . deny knowledge,' said Kant, 'in order to make room for faith.' But knowledge is *de facto* limited: not only because we can never know everything, that goes without saying, but because the essential always eludes us. We are as ignorant of the first cause as we are of the ultimate goal. Why is there something rather than nothing? We do not know. We will never know. Why? To what purpose? We do not know, nor even whether there is a purpose. But if it is true that nothing is born of nothing, the very existence of something – the world, the universe – would seem to imply that there has always been something: that being is eternal, uncreated, perhaps creator, and this is what some people call God.

Has He existed for all time? It would be more accurate to say that He exists out of time, creating it as he created all things. What did God do before the creation? He did nothing, according to St Augustine, but in truth there is no *before* (since any 'before' presupposes the existence of time): there was only the 'unending today' of God, which is neither day (what sun was there to measure it, since every sun depends on Him?), nor night, but something which precedes and contains every day, every night that we live, that we will live and all the numberless days and nights when there was no one living. Eternity is not contained in time; time is contained within eternity. God is not in the universe; the universe is in God. Should we believe? It seems the least we can do. Without this absolutely necessary being, nothing would have a reason to exist. How could He not exist?

God is outside the world, its cause and its end. Everything comes from him, everything is contained within Him ('it is in Him that we have being, movement and life', according to St Paul), everything tends towards Him. He is the *alpha* and the *omega* of being: the absolute Being – absolutely infinite, absolutely perfect, absolutely real – without which nothing relative could exist. Why is there something rather than nothing? *Because God*.

It may be said that this does not answer the question (why God rather than nothing?), and this is quite true.

But God would be the Being which answers the question of His own existence. He is His own cause, as philosophers put it, and this mystery (how can a being be its own cause?) is part of what defines Him. 'By cause of itself I understand that whose essence involves existence,' wrote Spinoza, 'or, that whose nature cannot be conceived except as existing.' This applies only to God; it is God. At least, it is the god of philosophers. 'How does God come to be in philosophy?' wonders Heidegger. As His own cause, Heidegger replies: 'the being of being, in the fundamental sense, cannot be conceived as a *causa sui*. To do so is to introduce the metaphysical concept of God.' Heidegger adds that Man 'cannot pray to this God nor make sacrifice to Him'. But without Him, no prayer, no sacrifice would be philosophically imaginable. What is God? God is a being which is absolutely necessary (self-causing), absolutely creator (the cause of everything), absolutely absolute (He is dependent on nothing, everything is dependent on Him): He is the Being of beings, and the foundation of all.

Does He exist? He exists by definition, though we cannot take that definition as a proof. This is what is both fascinating and irritating about the *ontological proof,* which – at least from St Anselm to Hegel – dominates Western philosophy. How to define God? The supreme being (St Anselm: 'that than which nothing greater can be thought'), that supremely perfect being (Descartes), that being which is absolutely infinite (Spinoza, Hegel).

But, if He did not exist, He would not be supreme, nor truly infinite and thereby lack some part of his perfection (to say the least!). He therefore exists by definition· to think God (to conceive Him as supreme, perfect, infinite . . .) is to think Him as existing. 'Existence cannot be separated from the essence of God,' writes Descartes, 'any more than an isosceles triangle from its two equal angles, or the idea of a mountain from the idea of a valley; it is no more repugnant to think of a God (that is to say a perfect being) as lacking existence (that is to say lacking perfection), than to conceive a mountain which has no valley.' It might be said that this does not prove that mountains and valleys exist . . . Certainly, agrees Descartes, but the idea of mountains and of valleys cannot be separated from one another. The same is true of God: His existence is inseparable from His essence, inseparable from Him, hence He necessarily exists. The concept of God, Hegel later writes, 'includes within it His existence': God is the only being who exists *in essence*.

Clearly, the ontological proof proves nothing: otherwise we would all be believers – something experience alone is sufficient to disprove – or fools – which it is not sufficient to prove. In any case, how can a definition prove anything whatsoever? One might as well claim to be wealthier by defining wealth . . . 'A hundred actual [francs] do not contain the least bit more than a hundred possible ones,' Kant remarks; but I am richer if I have one hundred real francs 'than with the mere concept of them (i.e. their possibility)'. It is not enough to define a sum of money to possess it. It is not sufficient to define God to prove that He exists. In any case, how can one prove an existence from a concept? It seems to me that the world is a better (not *a priori* but *a posteriori*) argument: what is known as the *cosmological proof*.

What is this? It is the application of the principle of sufficient cause to the world itself. 'No fact,' writes Leibniz, 'could be true or existent, no statement could be true unless there is sufficient cause that it should be so and not otherwise.' That is to say that it ought to be possible to explain everything that exists in principle, even where we are incapable of doing so in practice. And yet the world exists without explanation (it is contingent in that it could have not existed). Therefore, in order to explain its existence, we must postulate a cause. But if that cause, too, were contingent, it would in turn have to be explained by another, and so on *ad infinitum*, such that the whole series of causes – and therefore the world – would remain unexplained. Therefore, in order to explain all contingent beings (the world), we must postulate an absolutely necessary being (God). It follows, Leibniz goes on, that the final reason of things must be in a necessary substance in which the variety of particular changes exists only eminently, as in its source; and this substance we call *God*. To put it in other words: *If the world, then God; the world is, therefore God.*

To my mind this proof *a contigentia mundi* (from the

contingency of the world) as expressed by Leibniz (though it is also that of Thomas Aquinas and, to an extent, of Aristotle) is the most compelling, the most troubling, the only proof which occasionally makes me waver. Contingency is an abyss in which it is easy to lose your footing. How could it have no end, no cause, no reason?

However the cosmological proof is based entirely on the principle of reason. How can a principle prove anything whatever? To try to prove the existence of God from the contingency of the world is still to move from a concept (that of necessary cause) to an existence (that of God) and in this, as Kant noted, the cosmological proof boils down to the same thing as the ontological proof. Why should our reason be the norm? How can we be absolutely certain of its value, its scope, its trust-worthiness? Only God could warrant such things. Which is why it is impossible rationally to prove that He exists; since in order to guarantee the truth of our reasoning, we would have to presuppose the existence of God, whose existence we are attempting to prove. We step back from the abyss only to find ourselves in a vicious circle: we move from one trap to another.

At best, the cosmological proof proves no more than the existence of a necessary being. How can we be sure that such a being is, in the everyday sense of the word, a *God*? It could be Nature, as Spinoza contends, an infinite, eternal being, but one which has neither subjectivity nor personality: a being with no consciousness, no will, no love, a being which no one would regard as a satisfactory God. Why pray to Him, if He cannot listen? Why obey Him if He asks nothing of us? Why love Him if He does not love us?

From this springs the third of the traditional proofs for the existence of God: the *physio-theological proof*, which I prefer to call the *physio-teleological* proof (from the Greek *telos*: the purpose, the aim). The world is too ordered, too harmonious, too obviously *complete* for us to be able to explain it without postulating a benevolent, methodical intelligence as its cause. How could mere chance create a world so beautiful? How could it account for the appearance of life, its incredible complexity, its observable designs? If we were to find a watch on another planet, no one could believe that it was created solely by the laws of nature: everyone would see it as the result of intelligent, deliberate action. And yet, the least living thing is infinitely more complex than the most sophisticated watch. How could chance, which cannot explain the former, explain the latter?

Scientists may one day be able to provide an answer. But it's striking to note that this argument – long the most popular and the most immediately convincing (it was Cicero's view, and later that of Voltaire and Rousseau) – has lost much of its force. The harmony has begun to fall apart – witness the randomness of the universe, the horrors of the world – and what remains becomes easier to explain (by the laws of nature, by chance, necessity, evolution and the natural selection of species, by the immanent rationality of everything . . .). There can be no watch without a watchmaker, according to Voltaire and Rousseau. But it is a sorry sort of watch that includes earthquakes, hurricanes, droughts, carnivorous animals, numberless diseases – and Man! Nature is cruel, unjust, indifferent. How can we see the hand of God in such a thing? This is what is traditionally called 'the problem of evil'. To consider it a *mystery* – as most believers do – is to acknowledge that we are incapable of resolving it; the physio-theological proof thereby loses much of its impact. Too much suffering (long before man existed: animals suffer too), too much carnage, too much injustice. Certainly life is a marvel of engineering, but it is also a terrifying litany of tragedies and horrors. The fact that millions of animals feed on millions of others makes for a certain sort of equilibrium in the biosphere, but at the price of what atrocities for the living? The fittest survive; all others disappear. This makes for a certain sort of selection among species. But at the cost of pain and injustice for individuals. Natural history is hardly an edifying spectacle. Nor is human history. What God after Darwin? What God after Auschwitz?

The ontological proof, the cosmological proof and the physio-theological proof . . . these are traditionally the three great proofs for the existence of God and I could hardly have failed to mention them in this chapter.

Nonetheless we are forced to conclude that they prove nothing, as Kant has adequately demonstrated and as Pascal before him recognized. This did not prevent either of these geniuses from believing in God, or rather it made their belief what it is: faith, not knowledge; a grace or a hope, not a theorem. Both believed all the more fervently in God as they abandoned their attempts to prove His existence. Their faith was stronger, subjectively, in knowing that objectively it could not be verified.

This remains the rule today. I know few philosophers who are interested in these proofs for anything other than historical reasons, nor believers who hold to them as proofs. If there were proof, what need would we have of faith? Would a God whose existence was demonstrable still be a God?

This should not prevent us from considering the problem of God, examining the proofs, nor from devising others. For example, it is possible to imagine a purely *pantheistic* proof (from the Greek *pan*: everything) for the existence of God. Let us say that God is everything that exists: therefore, once again, he exists by definition (since everything that exists necessarily exists). But such a proof is of no significance, since it gives us no information as to His nature or His value. The universe could make a plausible God only if the universe itself could believe it. But can it? 'God,' my friend Marc Wetzel once told me, 'is the consciousness of Everything.' Perhaps. But what proof have we that Everything has a consciousness?

What is common to all of these proofs is that they

prove both too much and too little. Even if they prove the existence of something necessary, absolute, eternal, infinite, etc., they fail to prove that this 'something' is a God in the sense in which most religions use the word: not simply a being but a person, not only a reality but a cause, not only something but someone – not only a Principle but a Father.

This is the weakness of deism, too: it is belief without worship, without dogma. 'I believe in God,' a woman wrote to me, 'but not in the God of religions, which is simply human. The true God is unknowable . . .' All well and good. But if we know nothing whatever about Him, how do we know He is God?

To believe in God presupposes at least some knowledge of Him, which is possible only through reason, revelation, or grace. But reason increasingly acknowledges itself to be ineffectual. This leaves revelation and grace: which leaves religion . . . Which religion? From our present point of view it makes little difference, since philosophy has no way of choosing between them. The philosopher's God matters less to most of us than the God of the prophets, the mystics or the believers. Pascal and Kierkegaard cut to the essential more effectively than Descartes or Leibniz: God is an object of faith rather than of thought, or rather, not an object at all but a subject, giving himself only through revelation and love. Pascal believed he had such an experience one fiery night: 'God of Abraham, God of Isaac, God of Jacob, not of philosophers and scholars.

Certainty, heartfelt joy, peace. God of Jesus Christ . . .
Joy, joy, joy, tears of joy.' This is not a proof. But no proof,
without such experience, could equal faith.

This is where philosophy ends, perhaps. What need is
there to prove that which has been revealed? How can
you prove something which has not been revealed to
you? Being is not a predicate – Kant is right on this point
– and this is why, as Hume says, one cannot either prove
or disprove an existence. Being affirms rather than proves
itself; it is proof, but is not proven.

One might say that experience is proof. But experience
is not proof since it is neither repeatable, verifiable,
measurable, nor even entirely communicable . . .
Experience proves nothing, since some experiences are
false or illusory. Visions and ecstasies? Drugs can
induce similar states, and what proof can be had from
drugs? How do we know whether someone who sees
God actually is seeing or hallucinating? How do we
know if someone who hears God actually hears, or
speaks in His stead? How can we know whether those
who experience His presence, His love, His grace truly
experience something or simply imagine it? I don't
know a single believer more certain of the truth of his
faith than I am of my dreams. Certainty, inasmuch as it
is purely subjective, proves nothing. It is what we
call faith: 'a faith which is only subjectively sufficient,'
Kant writes, and which one cannot therefore impose –
either in theory or in practice – on another.

To put it another way, God is more mystery than

concept, more question than fact, more a wager than an experience, more a hope than a thought. God is what we postulate to overcome despair (according to Kant, this is the purpose of the postulates of practical reason) and it is why hope, like faith, is a theological virtue – since it postulates God as its object. 'The opposite of despair is faith,' wrote Kierkegaard: God is the only possible being who can completely satisfy our hope.

In conclusion, we must acknowledge that this, too, proves nothing: hope is not an argument, since it is possible, as Renan said, that the truth is cheerless. But what use are arguments which leave no room for hope?

What do we hope? That love is stronger than death, as it says in the *Song of Songs*, stronger than hatred, stronger than violence, stronger than anything, that this alone is truly God: love all-powerful, the love which saves, the one God – since he would be absolutely loving – who is truly loveable. It is the God of saints and mystics: 'God is love,' wrote Bergson, 'and the object of love: herein lies the whole contribution of mysticism. About this twofold love the mystic will never have done talking. His description is interminable, because what he wants to describe is ineffable. But what he does state clearly is that divine love is not a thing of God: it is God Himself.'

One might object that God is less a *truth* (the object of knowledge) than a *value* (the object of a desire). Probably. But to believe in him is to believe that this supreme value (love) is also the supreme truth (God). It cannot be proven. It cannot be refuted. But it can be thought, hoped, believed. God is truth as the standard – the conjunction of Truth and Goodness – and in that capacity the standard for all truths. At this highest level, what is desirable and what is intelligible are identical, explains Aristotle, and it is this *identity*, if it exists, which is God. How better to explain that He alone can fulfil or console us absolutely? 'Only a God could save us,' Heidegger admits. We must therefore believe – or renounce salvation.

We should note that this is why God has meaning and gives meaning: firstly, because without Him all meaning falters on the madness of death; secondly, because there can be meaning only for a subject and absolute meaning only for an absolute subject. God is the meaning of meaning, and in that sense the opposite of absurdity or despair.

Does He exist? We cannot know. God would be the answer to the question of being, to the question of truth, to the question of goodness, and these three answers – or three persons – would be one.

But being does not answer: that is what we call the world.

But truth does not answer: that is what we call thought.

Goodness? It has not answered yet, and that is what we call hope.

8: *Atheism*

'Faith saves, therefore it lies.

Nietzsche

Atheism is a singular thing in philosophy. It is a belief,
but a negative one. A thought, but one which feeds
entirely on the absence of its object.

This is clear from the etymology of the word: the small,
negative *a* next to the immensity of *theos* (god) . . . To be
an atheist is to be *without god*, either because one is
content not to believe in one or because one affirms that
none exists. In a monotheistic world such as ours we can
therefore distinguish two separate forms of atheism: not
believing in God (negative atheism) or believing that God
does not exist (positive or militant atheism). Absence of
belief or belief in absence. The absence of God or the
negation of God.

We won't dwell on the differences between these two

atheisms: they are separate currents rather than separate rivers; two poles but within one field. Between the two, all non-believers place themselves, hesitate, fluctuate . . . They are atheists nonetheless. You either believe in God or you don't: an atheist is any person who chooses the latter.

Agnostics are those who refuse to choose. This brings their position close to what I have called negative atheism, but – it is their hallmark – more open to the possibility of God. It amounts to a metaphysical centrism, or a religious scepticism. The agnostic does not commit himself, does not take a stand. He is neither believer nor non-believer: he leaves the problem unresolved. He has excellent reasons for doing so. Once we admit that we do not know whether God exists (if we knew, the question would not arise), why pronounce on his existence? Why affirm or deny something one cannot know? Here, too, etymology is enlightening. *Agnôstos*, in Greek, is the unknown or the unknowable. In religious terms, agnostics are those who do not know whether God exists and hold to that ignorance. Why should we reproach them for this? Humility seems to be on their side. Simplicity seems to side with them. In Protagoras' beautiful passage: 'Concerning the gods I cannot say either that they exist or that they do not, or what they are like in form; for there are many hindrances to knowledge: the obscurity of the subject and the brevity of human life.' It goes without saying that it is a respectable position, it seems a sensible one. It refers both believer and atheist back to their common excesses: both assert more than they can know.

But agnosticism's strength is also its weakness. If to be agnostic were simply to be ignorant of whether or not God exists, we would all be agnostics. In this sense, agnosticism would not be a philosophical position but a part of the human condition. Someone who tells you: 'I know that God does not exist' is a fool not an atheist. Let us say a fool who takes non-belief for knowledge. Similarly, someone who tells you: 'I know that God exists' is a fool who believes. The truth, and I must emphasize this, is that we do not know. Belief and non-belief are not proofs, that is their defining quality: when you know something, you no longer have to decide whether to nor to believe. Hence, as philosophers put it, agnosticism loses in understanding what it gains in ubiquity. If everyone is agnostic, why bother to claim to be one?

Agnosticism only becomes philosophically relevant when it, too, goes further than simply affirming its ignorance: when it asserts that such an affirmation is sufficient, or is better than the other position. It is choosing not to choose. This clearly highlights what atheism is: a choice, one which can be negative (not believing in God) or positive (believing that God does not exist), but one which takes a position, which engages with the question, which answers where agnosticism – its strength and its weakness – its content to leave the question open.

The agnostic does not take sides. The atheist does: he sides against God, or rather against His existence.

Why atheism? It is something which cannot be proven – atheists have often been more lucid on the subject than believers. There are no equivalents in the history of atheism of the famous, supposed 'proofs for the existence of God' . . . How do you prove non-existence? How could you prove that Santa Claus does not exist? That ghosts do not exist? How can you prove conclusively that God does not exist? How can our reason prove that nothing surpasses it? How can it refute something which, by definition, is beyond its comprehension? Even so, the fact that it is impossible does not condemn us to ignorance, nor is it an excuse for not considering the question. There is no proof, but there are arguments. Since I am an atheist, I would like to outline some of them.

The first is very simple, and wholly negative: a convincing reason to be an atheist is the weakness of the opposing arguments. Not only the weakness of the 'proofs', but the weakness of the revelations. If God existed, we should see or feel it more clearly! Why should God hide Himself? Believers respond that He does so to preserve our freedom: if God showed Himself in all His glory, we would no longer be free to decide whether to believe . . .

I don't find this answer satisfying. Firstly, because if it were true, then we are more free than God (how could the poor thing doubt His own existence?) and a number of his prophets (who are supposed to have encountered him in person), an implication which, philosophically and theologically, is hard to swallow.

Secondly, because one is always less free in ignorance than in knowledge. Should we stop teaching children in order to preserve their freedom? Every teacher and every parent believes the contrary: they believe that the more children know, the more they will be free! Ignorance is never freedom; knowledge is never slavery.

Lastly, and most importantly, because the argument seems to me incompatible with the orthodox view of God the Father. Clearly, I should respect my children's freedom. They are free to love or not to love me, to obey or disobey me, to respect me or not to respect me, which implies . . . that at least they know that I exist! A father who, in order to respect his children's freedom, refused to live with them, to be with them and even to be known to them would be a pitiful excuse for a father! Revelation? In raising his children, what father would be happy to send them word through others who have been dead for centuries, handed down through ambiguous and debatable texts? What father would send his children to read his selected works or those of his disciples (and which? The Bible? The Koran? The Upanishads?), rather than speaking to them directly and holding them to his heart? A peculiar father: a peculiar God! What father would hide from his children while they suffer? What father would hide himself from Auschwitz, from

Rwanda, when his children are sick or frightened? The *hidden God* of Pascal and Isaiah would be a bad father indeed. How could one love Him? How could one believe in Him? Atheism makes a more compelling hypothesis. If God cannot be perceived, and His absence cannot be understood, perhaps it is simply because He does not exist . . .

The second argument is also negative but, if I can put it like that, less empirical than theoretical. The principal role of God in human thought is to explain the world, life, to explain thought itself . . . But what use is such an explanation if God, should He exist, is by definition unexplainable? I do not deny that religion is a possible belief system. It goes without saying that it is highly regarded. But I wonder about the quality of its thinking. What is a religion if not a doctrine which seeks to explain something we do not understand (the existence of the universe, of life, of thought . . .) by means of something we understand even less (God)? And from a rational point of view, what is such an explanation worth? This is Spinoza's 'asylum of ignorance', and it applies just as much to his conception of God. In the *Ethics*, he writes: 'God, that is to say a substance constituted by an infinity of attributes each of which expresses an eternal or infinite essence, necessarily exists.' But what do we know of such a God or of the infinity of infinite attributes? Nothing, other than those attributes which resemble our ideas (scope, thought), which do not make up a God.

Why then believe? Freud has the answer to this: 'Ignorance is ignorance; no right to believe anything can be derived from it.' Or rather, we have the right to believe, but that cannot take the place of knowledge. Long live scepticism. Ignorance is no justification for faith, nor, inasmuch as it concerns God, can reason refute ignorance.

In that case, using God to explain anything (and, *a fortiori*, in an attempt to explain everything) explains nothing whatever, it simply replaces one form of ignorance with another. What's the point?

'I'm not an atheist,' a friend said to me, 'I believe there is mystery . . .' So? Does being an atheist involve negating the existence of mystery? Does the atheist claim to know everything, understand everything, explain everything? That would not be atheism but scientism, blindness, idiocy. Even if we could explain everything in the universe – and we have quite a way to go – we would still have to explain the universe itself, something we could not do. We would still have to judge, to love, to act, to live, things which no science could ever encompass. This is what distinguishes atheism from scientism, which is a blinkered form of atheism. Scientism is a religion of the sciences: it is not the essence of atheism, of materialism or of rationalism; it is a dogmatic and fossilized quasi-religious caricature of these things. We might call it the religion of non-believers: a system of 'free thought' almost incompatible with a thought that is free!

Obviously science cannot explain everything, reason

cannot explain everything. There are things we do not know and things we do not understand, there is mystery and there always will be. Scientists are wrong to claim otherwise. But what right have believers to monopolize mystery, to appropriate it, to make it their domain? The fact that mystery exists does not make religion right or reason wrong! It means that dogmatism, whether religious or rationalist, is wrong. Which is damning for religion, since it relies entirely on dogma. A scientist need not worship science, but what believer does not worship his God?

To be an atheist is not a refusal of mystery; it is a refusal to push it aside or take the easy way out by an act of faith or of submission. Atheism is not an attempt to explain everything, but a refusal to explain everything by means of the unexplainable.

On the other hand, believing in God does not add mystery to the world; it simply gives a name (even if unpronounceable) to that mystery and reduces it neatly to a story of power or family, of covenant or love . . . God almighty, God the creator, God the merciful judge – 'Our father which art in heaven . . .' This explains everything, but by means of something which itself cannot be explained. Consequently, it explains nothing; it simply relocates the mystery – almost always in anthropomorphism. 'In the beginning God created the heavens and the earth, and man after his own image . . .' This explains the universe in terms of something which resembles us, or which we resemble. 'If God created us in his image,' wrote Voltaire, 'we have amply returned the favour.' Psychologically, what could be more comprehensible? Philosophically, what could be more dubious? The universe is more mysterious than either the Bible or the Koran. How can what is contained within these books explain it?

The smallest flower presents an unfathomable mystery. But why should we hope to find the solution to that mystery through faith?

What is essential is unknowable to us. But why should we wish that unknowable to be God?

The three other arguments are more positive. The first is the most trivial and the most compelling: the problem of evil. There is too much horror in the world, too much suffering and injustice for us to easily believe that it was created by a God who is absolutely good and all-powerful.

The following paradox is well known and dates back to Epicurus and Lactance: either God wishes to wipe out evil and cannot, in which case he is not all-powerful, or he could do so but chooses not to, in which case he is not perfectly good . . . But if he is not both (and, more importantly, if he is neither), can he still be God? This is the problem of all theodicy, as Leibniz frames it: 'If God exists, whence comes evil? If he does not exist, whence comes goodness?' But the problem evil poses to faith is more serious than that which good poses to atheism. It is more categorical, more infinite, more implacable. When a child smiles, we hardly need a god to explain it. But when a child dies, or suffers terribly, who would dare praise the glory of God and His creation to the mother of that child? Yet how many children suffer terribly every minute all over the world?

Believers answer that Man himself is responsible for many of these horrors . . . This is true. But he is not the cause of all of them, nor of himself. Freedom does not explain everything. Sin does not explain everything. One is reminded of Diderot's great quip: 'The Christian god is a father who makes much of his apples, and very little of his children.' This is just as valid for the God of the Jews and the Muslims. It is just as damning to any God who is supposed to be a god of love and mercy – and how could He be God if He were otherwise? Why should we accept in Him things we would not find acceptable in a father? I have spent many hours in the paediatric unit of a large Paris hospital. It leaves one with rather a high opinion of mankind. And rather a low opinion of God, if He exists. 'The suffering of children,' wrote Marcel Conche, quite correctly, 'is an absolute evil,' which in itself renders all theodicy impossible. How many atrocities have there been which no human fault would be sufficient to explain? How much suffering preceded the first sin? How many horrors precede the existence of humanity itself. Who is this God who abandons gazelles to tigers and children to cancer?

The second argument is more subjective, and I offer it as such: I do not have a sufficiently high opinion of humanity in general nor of myself in particular to believe that a god created us. Such great power to such little effect! There is too much mediocrity, too much baseness, too much *misery*, as Pascal said, and too little greatness.

This is not to say that we should add to it. All misanthropy is iniquitous: it supposes that heroes do not exist, that good people do not exist and leaves the world to evildoers and to cowards. But heroes too have their petty foibles which make them human. Neither one nor the other requires God to be conceivable. Courage is enough. Kindness is enough. Humanity is enough. What god, on the other hand, could justify the hatred, violence, cowardice and idiocy which are everywhere? Leaving aside the monster and the villain, a little self-knowledge, as Bergson realized, is sufficient for us to be more contemptuous than admiring of Man. Humanity displays too much selfishness, vanity and fear. Too little courage and generosity. Too much *amour propre*, too little love. Humanity is such a pitiful creation, how could God want *this*?

Religion, all religion, is narcissistic (if God created me, then I am worthy), which in itself is reason to be atheist: to believe in God is to commit the sin of pride.

Atheism, on the other hand, is a form of humility. It is to think of ourselves as animals, which indeed we are, and leave to us the responsibility of *becoming* human. It might be said that this *responsibility* was given us by God, in order to enable us continue His creation . . . Perhaps.

But the burden is too heavy and the gate too strait for me to be satisfied with this answer. Insignificant beings that we are, Nature seems to me cause enough.

The third positive argument may seem surprising. If I do not believe in God it is also, perhaps especially, because I would rather that He did exist. This is something of an inversion of Pascal's wager. It is not important that an idea be advantageous to us – thought is not a business or a lottery – but that it should be plausible. And yet God seems to me to be less *plausible* than he is *advantageous*: He accords so closely to our keenest desires that we have to wonder whether we did not create him to that end.

What do we desire more than anything? Not to die, to be reunited with loved ones we have lost, to be loved . . . And what does Christianity tell us? That we will not die, or not really, that we will be raised up again; secondly, that we will be reunited with the loved ones we have lost; lastly that we are now and will for ever be loved with an infinite love . . . What more could we ask? Nothing, obviously: that's what makes religion improbable! By what miracle would reality, so atypically, accord so perfectly with our desires? This does not prove that God does not exist – since He, by definition, could make such a miracle possible – but it does make one wonder whether God isn't too good to be true, whether we are not simply deluding ourselves, whether religion is not simply an *illusion*, in the Freudian sense of the word: not necessarily an error (it is possible, after all, that God exists), but 'a belief derived from human wishes'. Though this does not refute the existence of God, it makes the possibility of his existence more tenuous. 'We shall tell ourselves that it would be very nice if there were a God who created the world and was a benevolent Providence, and if there were a moral order in the universe and an after-life; but it is a very striking fact that all this is exactly as we are bound to wish it to be.' To believe in God is to believe in Santa Claus to the power of a thousand, or rather to the power of infinity. It is to provide ourselves with a surrogate Father who will console us for the failings or the loss of our actual fathers, He will be true Justice, true Love, true Power, and He will accept us and love us for what we are, He will fulfil us, He will save us . . . I can well understand why we might wish for such a thing. But why should we believe in it? 'Faith saves,' said Nietzsche, 'therefore it lies.' Let us simply admit that God is a little too convenient for us not to find Him suspect.

Suppose I say to you: 'I'm looking to buy a three-bedroom flat in Paris behind the Jardin du Luxembourg with a magnificent view of the park . . . I don't want to spend more than €10,000; but I'm confident, I believe!' Obviously you'd think: 'He's deluding himself; he's confusing what he wants with what he can get . . .' Obviously, you'd be right (though that, strictly speaking, proves nothing: who knows whether I'll come across some crazy person willing to sell to me?). And yet when I tell you that God exists, that we will be resurrected, etc., you don't find that a little more unbelievable than a three-bedroom flat with a flat with a view of the Jardin du Luxembourg for less than ten grand? Either you have a very poor opinion of God, or a very high one of real estate!

The position of the atheist is reinforced by the fact that, as often as not, he would like to be wrong. This does not prove that he is right, but it leaves him less open to the suspicion that, like others, he believes simply to console or reassure himself . . .

I shall stop here. I intended only to outline a number of possible arguments. Each of you can weigh up their strengths and limitations. It is not rationally possible to exclude the possibility that God exists. This is what makes atheism what it is: not knowledge, let me repeat, but belief, not a certainty, but a wager.

It is this which should encourage us to be tolerant. Atheists and believers are separated only by a shared ignorance. How could this be more important than the knowledge they share: a certain experience of life, of love, of suffering humanity, dignified in spite of its misery, suffering but courageous? This is what I call faithfulness, something which should bring together those whose faith or lack of faith might otherwise pit them against one another. It would be madness to kill one another over something we do not know. It is better for us to fight together for those things we know or acknowledge: a certain conception of mankind and of civilization, a certain way of living in the world, in its mysteries, a certain rigorousness of mind . . . This is what we might call humanism, which is not a religion, but a morality. Faithfulness to mankind and to the humanity of mankind.

This cannot replace a God. Nor can it eliminate a God. But without this faith no possible religion nor any form of atheism could be humanly acceptable.

9: Art

'What we seek in art as in thought is truth.'

Hegel

Art is a product of man. Neither a bird's nest nor its song
are works of art any more than are the hive or the dance
of the bee. It is not beauty which distinguishes them.
What figurative painter would claim that his works are
more beautiful than those of nature, which he can
imitate but never equal? What abstract painter could
better the sky or the sea? What sculptor could better life,
or the wind? And how many musicians are less easy on
the ear, alas, than the lowliest nightingale?

Beauty is one of the possible aims of art; but in itself it is
not sufficient to define it. Nature, too, is beautiful –
more beautiful. If man alone is an artist, it is not
primarily because he is an artisan (an ape can also make

tools), nor an aesthete (who can tell whether the peahen feels some sort of aesthetic pleasure when gazing at the tail of the peacock?), nor even through the union of these two faculties. A work of art is not simply the beautiful end-product of an activity, nor is every beautiful object a work of art. There must be something else, which Nature, without Man, is lacking, and which undoubtedly no other animal perceives. What? Humanity itself, inasmuch as it questions itself and the world; inasmuch as it seeks truth or meaning; inasmuch as it questions and interprets; inasmuch as it reasons, if you like; let us say that Man can depict Nature as it presents itself only on condition that he projects himself into it, on to it, that he 'finds' himself within it, as Hegel puts it, which implies – since Nature neither asks nor answers – that he transforms or re-creates it. This can be done without art. But art does it better and more profoundly. This is because the mind is less distracted by its usual goals, which are function, power, efficiency. It is because the artist, seeking only to imitate the world, has no other model – since the world does not imitate itself – than he himself as he imitates it. If it were sufficient simply to look, painting would be easy. But would it be art? In music, what model could the artist work from, other than the work itself as it unfolds, other than a certain idea which is neither concept nor word. Consider Rembrandt, consider Mozart. This is not the beauty of this world. This is not the truth of this world. Or if it is of this world, it is so only because it is Mozart's or

Rembrandt's. 'The things of Nature are content to *be*,' wrote Hegel, 'they simply *are*, they exist only once; but Man, through consciousness, splits in two: he exists once, but he also exists *to himself*.' This is why he needs art: to 'externalize what he is' and to find in it 'a reflection of himself'. Anyone for whom the world, without Man, is sufficient should not be here.

In art, humanity contemplates itself in the act of contemplating; questions itself questioning; recognizes itself in the act of recognizing. This reflexivity, when it is incarnate, tangible, is art. 'All arts are like mirrors,' according to Alain, 'in which Man learns and recognizes something of himself of which he was unaware.' Probably. Not because in art Man looks only at himself. Rather because he cannot look at anything whatever – unless he loses himself completely – without being aware of himself in the act of looking. The true mirror in which Man searches for himself is the world. Art is merely the reflection in which he finds himself.

Should the artist imitate nature? It is only one of many possibilities. The old Greek dilemma of *mimesis* (imitation), as enlightening as it is, is both partial and simplistic: it could not apply to all the arts, nor to all art. Imitation has little place in music or in architecture, nor in a large part of contemporary painting or sculpture. And what does it matter if a painter, a novelist, a film-maker imitates nature, if he brings us something new, something pleasing or stirring? A work of art, according to Kant, is not the representation of a beautiful object, but 'a beautiful representation of an object'. Look at Van Gogh's *Shoes*, Chardin's *La Raie* or Goya's Black Paintings . . . . These are not imitations of what is beautiful, which hardly needs imitating; they celebrate beauty where it exists; create or reveal it when it is absent or unremarked. This is something of which photography forcibly reminds us. Any snapshot is a reasonable likeness. But how many photographs are art? How many are valuable in themselves? Imitation is often a means or a requirement of art. But it is only a means, not an end. It is only one requirement among others, often stimulating, often true, often salutary, but it is not a necessary requirement nor is it ever, in itself, sufficient. Imitating what is beautiful is a postcard aesthetic. An artist does not copy, he creates.

Kant brings us closer to the mystery. 'Beautiful art is art of genius', he writes. But what is genius? '. . . the talent (natural gift) that gives the rule to art', according to Kant. It doesn't matter whether this creative force is innate, as Kant would have it, or acquired – it must be one or the other. What is important, and what makes Kant right, is that it creates the rules of art only through creating art 'for which no determinate rule can be given'. Genius is the opposite of a set of instructions, nonetheless it functions as just that. It cannot be reduced to any given set of rules (which is what distinguishes art from mere craft and genius from know-how), but through it the artist imparts rules – however implicit and mysterious they may be – to his successors. In art, genius is that which cannot be learned and yet can teach. That which does not imitate and yet is imitated. This is why, as Malraux said, 'it is in museums that one learns to paint': because it is in admiring and imitating the masters that one may have a chance of becoming one oneself.

From this comes the paradox of genius, which is to be both original and exemplary. Original, since it cannot be reduced to a set of rules, to imitation or knowledge. But exemplary, too, since originality itself is not enough ('there can also be original nonsense', remarks Kant: something which prefigures some of the art of the twentieth century), since genius must also serve as a model, a reference, which means that works of art, ording to Kant, 'while not themselves the result of itation, they must yet serve others in that way, i.e., as standard or a rule for judging'. One can create any old rbbish, in art as in anything. But any old rubbish is not rt. There are mediocre artists, but they are not important. Only the genius makes the rules: art is only truly recognized in the exceptions, which are the only rule.

Great artists are those who combine singularity and universality, subjectivity and objectivity, spontaneity and discipline, and this is possibly the true miracle of art, which distinguishes it from technology and science. In every civilization which has used the bow, the arrow tends to be balanced at a point two-thirds along its length. This remarkable technical convergence, however, says nothing about humanity, nor about its intelligence, still less about the individuals concerned: it owes everything to the physical world and its laws. It is *invention*, not *creation*, and the inventor is of no significance. Without the Lumière brothers, we would still have had the cinema. But without Godard, we would never have had *Breathless* or *Pierrot le Fou*. Without Gutenberg, sooner or later we would have had the printing press. Without Villon, we would never had had *The Ballad of the Hanged Men*. Inventors save us time. Artists waste it — and save it.

This is also true of the sciences. Imagine if Newton or Einstein had died at birth. The history of the sciences would certainly have been very different, but in its rhythm rather than its content, in its detail rather than in its direction. Neither the laws of gravity nor the equivalence between mass and energy would have been lost: someone else would have discovered them later, and this is why they are *discoveries*, and not *creations*. But if Shakespeare had never existed, if Michelanglo or Cézanne had never existed, we would not have a single one of their works nor anything that might substitute for them. It would not only be the rhythm, the personalities or the history of art which would be different, but some of the most essential part of its content and, to some extent, its direction. What would Mozart have been without Haydn? Schubert without Beethoven? All of them without Bach? Geniuses move art forward, they constitute it, they are as irreplaceable after the fact as they are unpredictable before.

I should say in passing that the same is true of philosophy. Without Plato, without Descartes, without Nietzsche it would have been – and would still be – essentially different from the way we know it today. This is enough to prove that it is not a science. But is it art? It is a question of definition. But it is an art in the sense that it would not exist, or would be radically different, without a number of singular geniuses who were, as in art, original yet exemplary: it is they who serve as a measure and a rule, as Kant put it, in judging what a work of philosophy could and should offer. It is the art of reason, if you like, for which truth, even the possibility of truth, is beauty enough.

To return to the arts: traditionally, there are thought to be six, though the list has changed over time (currently: painting, sculpture, architecture, music, dance, literature) to which it has long been customary to add a 'seventh art', cinema, and in France even an eighth, which is the graphic novel. What do they have in common? Firstly, the subjectivity I mentioned earlier, by which a genius can attain the universal. Art expresses the 'irreplaceable in our lives', as Luc Ferry puts it, to which all arts contribute. But they also have in common the pleasing emotions they evoke in us independently of whether one possess them or whether they are useful. Who needs to own a Vermeer to delight in it, to be moved by it? Who needs anything more of Mozart than the pleasure – even when it is heart-rending – of listening to his music? To describe this disinterested pleasure we use the necessarily vague term beauty. It is not peculiar to art, but what art would there be without it?

Something is beautiful, explains Kant, if it is recognized as the object of disinterested pleasure (we tend to feel that by rights everyone should find beauty in what we ourselves judge to be beautiful), and which manifests a certain form of finality without any goal being manifest (there is a sense of completeness in a flower or in a work of art which seem to us all the more beautiful in that they are independent of an external purpose. I am not a Kantian, but I believe that there is no beauty without pleasure, which, for me, is an end in itself. Poussin thought likewise: 'The purpose of art is delectation,' as did Molière: 'The only rule is to please.' In fact art is the mind itself, delighting in what it loves.

What it loves or what it knows? Both, in fact, and it is this that makes art all the more precious. It teaches us to love truth, by bringing out the beauty of an object, even if the object itself is ugly or banal. Two apples, an onion, a pair of old shoes . . . A couple of notes, a couple of musical notes. And suddenly it is as if the Absolute itself were hanging on the wall or in the air, radiating in all its splendour, all its timelessness, all its truth, finally revealed, as though it had never been revealed before . . . 'Real life,' wrote Proust, 'life at last laid bare and illuminated – the only life in consequence which can be said to be really lived – is literature . . . This does not mean that books are better than life, nor that writers live life more intensely than we do. What it means, on the contrary, is that literature, like all of the arts, helps us to perceive and to inhabit this real life, which is, as Proust continues, 'all the time immanent in ordinary men no less than in the artist.' It is something which most people do not perceive through inattention or lack of ability but which the artist, in his singularity, reveals to us. Beauty is not sufficient. Still less ugliness, nor, despite Nietzsche, illusion. We need beauty, we need truth, even more do we need the confluence of the two, their fusion, their unity, and this is why we need artists: not to make life more beautiful to us, which would be no more than artifice or ornament, but to reveal to make manifest its intrinsic beauty, to teach us how to see it, to take pleasure in it and rejoice in it – to love it. It is not a question of prettifying, nor of creating a likeness. It is love without deceit – consider Mozart, consider Vermeer – that is true art.

'Art brings forth truth,' wrote Heidegger. 'In a single bound, art brings to the fore, as an established safeguard, the truth of existence.' Not the truth of science, with its concepts, theories and abstractions. Artistic truth is always concrete, always practical, always, in its way, silent (even when expressed in words or sounds): it is the truth of being, inasmuch as we are able to grasp it, it is – according to Heidegger – 'being in search of being itself', and as such it is the human, necessarily human, face of the Absolute which encompasses us, which is us. Too bad for the aesthetes and virtuosi if they are no more than that. Beauty is not everything; technique is not everything. Art is first and foremost revelation rather than craft or ability, it is the establishing or the implementation of a truth. And for Man, what truth can there be without language? What silence, even, without language? This is where poetry exists. Poetry, which is the essence of art in every art and its apotheosis because, as Heidegger again says: 'the essence of art is poetry', and because 'the essence of poetry is the stating of truth'.

If 'Man lives the world as a poet', it is thanks to those creators (in Greek, those *poiètai*) who have taught us to see it, to know it, to celebrate it – both to confront it and to transform it – to rejoice in it even when it is unpleasant, to rejoice in it or to bear it even when it is sad or cruel, in short to love it or to forgive it, since in the end we must, since that is the sole wisdom of mankind and of art. This is where the aesthetic encroaches on the ethical. 'For there is certainly something in the conception that the end of art is the beautiful,' wrote Wittgenstein. 'And the beautiful *is* what makes happy.' Not any form of beauty however, nor any form of happiness. In art, the only beauty which matters is that which does not lie.

I spoke earlier of what music would be like without Bach or Beethoven, or the plastic arts without Michelangelo or Rembrandt, literature without Shakespeare or Hugo . . . But surely it is obvious that without these incomparable artists – each universal, each singular – humanity itself would be other than it is.

Because it would be less beautiful, less cultured, less happy? This is not the only, nor the most important reason. Because it would be less true and less human. Art is a product of man. Man is a product of art.

10: Time

'Only the present exists.'

Chrysippus

What is time? 'If no one asks me, I know what it is,'
admitted St Augustine. 'If I wish to explain it to him
who asks, I do not know.' Time is both obvious and
mysterious: each of us experiences it; none can com-
prehend it. It runs on constantly. If it stopped, even for a
moment, everything would stop and there would no
longer be any time. There would no longer be anything at
all. No movement (since time is necessary for motion),
no rest (since time is necessary to remain stationary).
Without time, there would no longer be a present,
therefore there would be no 'there is': how then could
there be anything? Time, Kant demonstrates, is the *a
priori* prerequisite of all phenomena. In other words, to
us, it is the prerequisite of everything.

In any case, how could time stop, since any concept of stopping is contained with it? 'O Time, suspend your flight!' So pleads the poet according to Alain, but the plea 'falters if one asks: for how much time should Time suspend its flight?' Only one of two things is possible: either Time stops only *for a certain time*, in which case it has not stopped; or it stops definitvely, in which case the very concepts of 'stopping' or 'end' cease to have any meaning. There can be no stop except in relation to a *before*; something can be definitive only in relation to an *after*. But *before* and *after* presuppose the concept of time: the idea that time could stop, whether temporarily or permanently, can be conceived only within time itself.

For us, time is the horizon of being and of all beings. Eternity would be the contrary of time, something we cannot know, cannot think, cannot experience. As he walks among ruins, Diderot thinks: 'everything ceases to exist, everything perishes, everything passes away. Only the world continues. Time alone persists.' In fact, without time, nothing could remain, pass away, endure or even cease to exist. To be is to be in time, since it is either to continue or to cease. But what is time, which passes only if it remains, which remains only if it passes, which can be experienced only as it passes, thereby eluding us?

Time must be, since without it, nothing could be. But what is it?

What we call time is, primarily, the succession of the

past, the present and the future. But the past is not, since it is no longer. Nor the future, since it is not yet. As for the present, it appears to us as time – rather than eternity – only in that, moment by moment, it erases itself. 'Time is,' wrote St Augustine, 'only as it tends towards non-being'. This is what we call the present: the disappearance of the future into the past; what is not yet, engulfed by what is no longer. Is it between these two? The *passage* – elusive, insubstantial, of no duration – from one to the other, since all duration presupposes the notion of past and future which do not exist. It is transitory being (the present) flanked on either side by nothingness (the future, the past). A fleeing between two absences. A lightning flash flanked by night. How could such a thing make up the world? How could such a thing make up duration?

Let us consider the present moment. You are reading this short essay about time . . . What you were doing previously is in the past, is nothing, or almost nothing; let us say it is no longer: it exists only inasmuch as someone in the present remembers it. But that memory is not, nor can it be, the past: it is merely a trace of it or an evocation of it, both of which are part of the present. If your memory itself were in the past, you would no longer remember it: it would no longer be a memory, but something you had forgotten. The past exists for us only in the present, as part of the present: it exists – and this is the paradox of memory – only in that it is *not the past*.

Does this mean that a past which no one remembers

would be nothing, absolutely nothing? It is not that simple. For even though something is no longer it remains true – eternally true – that it *was*. A little girl cries; she is in Auschwitz, crying because she is cold, because she is hungry; a little girl who will be led to the gas chambers a few days later – let us say in December 1942. No one remembers her name or her face. It was too long ago; all of those who knew her are dead. Her body has disappeared; how could anyone remember her tears? True. But that which took place nevertheless remains true, and will always remain true, even if, today or tomorrow, there is no one to remember it. Each of her tears is an eternal truth, as Spinoza would put it, and without it there could be no truth. Does this mean that the past exists after all? No, because this truth, too, is present, is always the present: to the mind, eternity is nothing more than the ever-presence of truth. It is not that the past remains; it is that the truth does not pass away.

You have just read the previous sentences. They took up a few brief moments of your present, which you will quickly forget. Will it still be true that you read them? Probably; but it will also be true that you have forgotten them . . . In any case, even if you were to remember them for your whole life, those moments would still be definitively behind you. Though you might reread these pages tomorrow, or ten years from now, you can never recapture that moment which no longer exists, that moment when you first read them or when you last read them. Time will have continued to pass, to change, and that is the real mystery: the present continually ceases to exist (becomes the past) though it never disappears (because it persists). This mystery is time, which the past can neither contain nor dispel. How could the past be time, since it is no longer? How could time be past, since it persists?

The future? Your immediate future, most probably, will be to read the following sentences . . . But it cannot be certain, it is not yet: a friend might interrupt you, you might get bored, think about something else, mislay this book, you might even drop dead . . . If 'what is yet to be' existed, it would not be yet to be, it would be the present. It is what it is – and this is the paradox of anticipation – only on condition that it is not yet. It is not real; it is possible, virtual, imaginary. Will you read to the end of this chapter? You will know only when you have finished it: it will not then be the future, but the past. In the meantime? All you can do is to continue or stop: that is not the future, but the present. Hope, anticipation, imagination, resolve? All of these exist only in the present: they are present or not at all. Tomorrow, next year, ten years from now? This is the future only because it is not; it is possible only on condition that it is not real. You can skip a couple of pages, rush to the end of the book, but regardless of how fast you go, whether you go by train, plane or rocket, you can never escape the present, the real, time. You must pause or act and these things can be done only in the present. How could the future be in time, since it is not yet? How could time be the future, since time is always here, now, since it precedes us, accompanies us, contains us?

Time passes, but is not the past. It is yet to come, but is not the future. Nothing is past, nothing is to come, nothing is but the present.

And yet the present is the present only at the very instant that it slips into the past: try to catch it, it is already past; 'if it were always present, and never moved on to become the past,' remarks St Augustine, 'it would not be time but eternity.' But, the author of the *Confessions* continues, 'If, therefore, the present is time only by reason of the fact that it moves on to become the past, how can we say that even the present *is*, when the reason why it *is* is that it is *not to be*?' His conclusion takes the form of a paradox: 'In other words, we cannot rightly say that time *is*, except by reason of its impending state of *not being*.'

The paradox is perhaps less challenging than it might at first appear.

Firstly because St Augustine's objection (if the present were always present, it would not be time but eternity) supposes that time and eternity are mutually exclusive, something which is neither self-evident nor proven.

Secondly, because nothing proves that time passes into past time, nor even that such a thing is conceivable. Where could it do so, given that the past no longer exists? And how, since it can pass only in the present?

Finally, and most importantly, because St Augustine's

analysis – which has been exemplary up to this point – seems here to deviate from our experience. Have you ever observed the present cease to be? Does it change? Of course it does, but it can do so only on condition that it continues. It is true that what *was* is no longer present. But the present itself still exists. Have you ever experienced anything else? Since you were born, have you ever lived a single second of the past, or a millisecond of the future? Have you experienced anything other than the present, lived a single day that was not a *today*? In what sense can the present be said to 'cease to be', since nothing can cease to be unless the present continues? I am pretty certain I have never observed the present cease to be, it has always continued, endured, persisted. Thinking about it, the present is probably the only thing I have always had in abundance. I have often needed more money, sometimes needed more love, better health, more courage . . . but never more present. Like everyone else, I have often needed more time, but the time I needed was almost always in the future (what we refer to as urgency: when we don't have any time *ahead of us*), sometimes in the past (what we refer to as nostalgia: yearning for something which was) never the present: the present has always been here, present and correct!

How, then, is it possible to need more time when time itself is presupposed by any need? How is it possible to observe the present *cease to be* when the present is a prerequisite to sight, to cessation and to being?

The present never ceases, never commences. It does not come from the future any more than it disappears into the past: it persists and changes, it endures and transforms – and it can change or transform only because it endures and persists. 'Duration,' said Spinoza, 'is an indefinite continuation of existence.' It is time itself: the continuous present – always changing – of being. We must therefore invert St Augustine's maxim. 'Thus,' he wrote, 'can we not truly say that time *is* only as it tends toward nonbeing?' I believe the contrary to be true: we can truly say that time is, only as it tends towards persistence.

It might therefore be said that time and eternity are one. Why not? But we will return to that later.

The past is no longer, the future is not yet: there is only the present, which is the only real time. This, however, is not how we experience time. On the contrary, we are conscious of time only because we remember the past, because we anticipate the future, because we mark the difference between the two in our minds or with our clocks . . . With our clocks? But the movement of the clock's hands is simply a sliver of the present: it is not time, according to Bergson, it is space. Only the mind, which remembers the previous position of the hands of the clock, and anticipates their future position, can distinguish duration. Without the mind there would be nothing but a continuous present, without past or future: there would be only the current position of the hands, there would be only space. But the mind does play a role, because memory exists, because the body exists and remembers the past, the present and even (think of your appointments, your plans, your promises) the future. It is no longer space, but duration. It is no longer movement, but consciousness. It is no longer an instant, but an interval. This is why we can measure time (just try measuring the present!); why we distinguish between time and infinity (which would be pure present, without past or future); in short, it is why we are in time (and not simply in the present) – unless, perhaps, time is in us . . .

Why the hesitation? Because this thing called time – which we measure or imagine – is, for the most part, composed of the past and of the future, which exist only in the mind: how can we tell whether time itself exists only in the mind? Philosophically, this question – that of the objectivity or subjectivity of time – is an important one. Is time a part of the world, of nature, of reality in itself? Or does it exist only to us, only in our minds, only subjectively? It is possible that both are true – from different points of view – in other words, that there are two different times, or two different ways of thinking time: on the one hand, objective time – that of the world and of nature – which is a perpetual *now*, as Hegel puts it, and as such indivisible (just try to divide the present!); on the other, time as it pertains to consciousness and the mind, which is merely the sum – in and for the mind – of a past and a future. We can call the first *duration* and the second *time*. But only on condition that we do not forget that they are one and the same thing considered from two different viewpoints: that time is simply the human measure of duration. 'To determine duration,' wrote Spinoza, 'we compare it to the duration of things which have an invariable and determined duration, and this comparison we call time.' But no comparison can bring something into being. This is why it is important not to confuse duration and time, but to distinguish one from another as though both existed in isolation. This is not the case. Duration is part of reality, or rather it is reality: it is the indefinite continuance of its existence. Time, on the other hand, is simply a concept of the mind: it is the way in which we think of or measure the indivisible and infinite duration of everything.

Duration is a facet of being; time, in this sense, subjective. This latter, time experienced, subjective time (which alone allows us to *measure* objective time: a clock can exist only in consciousness), is what twentieth-century philosophers usually refer to as *temporality*. It is an aspect of consciousness rather than of the world. An extendedness of the mind, as St Augustine put it, rather than of the body. A form of *a priori* sensibility as Kant would say, rather than an intrinsic or objective reality. A facet of the subject, rather than the object. But the fact that we can experience time only through our subjectivity, as Kant or Husserl demonstrate, does not prove that it can be reduced merely to this, nor does it seem to me to be likely. For if time existed only for us, how could we have come to be in time? What reality can be attributed to the millions of years which are known to us (thanks to scientists, geologists, paleaontologists) only retrospectively, as the time which preceded us, the time before consciousness, which must certainly have preceded it and cannot have emerged from it? If time exists only to us, how could it have passed between the Big Bang and the appearance of life? And how, if it did not pass, could Nature have evolved, changed, shaped? If time were only subjective, how could subjectivity have come to appear in time?

Let us take an indeterminate period of time, let us say today. Some of that period has already passed, some is yet to come. As for the present – which separates the two – it is merely an instant of no duration (if it had duration it too would be made up of a past and a future), which is not in time. We experience this as time because our mind remembers what is no longer and anticipates what is not yet, it causes both to exist in the present – the present we experience – when in reality they could not coexist. Therefore, as Marcel Conche understood, temporality allows us to apprehend time only because it is a negation of time: Man resists time (because he remembers, because he anticipates); and in doing so he becomes conscious of it. The mind constantly resists; that is what the mind is: memory, imagination, obstinacy, will . . . But it is possible to resist time only with time. Memory, imagination, obstinacy, will, exist only within the present. The mind exists only in the body, in the world; that is what it means to exist. How can we conquer time, since we can wrestle with it only on condition that we are part of it?

Time is always the victor: because it is always there, because there is always time, because the present is the only 'there is' of being; in it all things pass, while it itself does not pass. This is why we grow old; it is why we die. Ronsard summed it up in two lines:

> Time goes by, time goes by, my Lady . . .
> Alas! Not time itself, but we go by!

Another good reason to make the most of youth, of life. But how?

By living in the present? We must do so because it is the only time given to us. By living in the moment? Absolutely not, to do so would be to abandon memory, imagination, will – to abandon the mind and the self. How could one possibly think without remembering our ideas; love without remembering those we love; act without remembering our desires, plans, dreams? When we study, or save for our retirement, we are planning our future – a wise thing to do. But it is in the present, not the future, that we study or save. If we keep our promises, it is first and foremost because we remember them, as we must. But it is in the present that we keep them, not in the past. Living in the present does not mean cutting ourselves off from the past, or from our desires, since both are part of it. It does not mean living in the moment, because we carry on, we endure, we grow up or grow old. No instant is a resting place for Man, only the present, which persists and changes; only the mind, which remembers and imagines. That the mind itself exists only in the present – in the brain – is obvious. We are of the world – that is our body – and we are *in* the world, that is our mind; the two, in my opinion, are one. But the world has no mind. And the mind is not the world. This is why we are constantly threatened by forgetfulness, death, exhaustion, idiocy and nothingness. To exist is to resist; to think is to create; to live is to act.

All of these things can take place only in the present – since there is nothing else – and it is succeeded only by another present. How could one live in the past or the future? To do so one would mean to no longer be, or to not yet be. Living in the present, as Stoics and sages have said, is not a dream, nor an ideal, nor a utopia: it is the simple and extremely difficult truth of being. If eternity is 'a perpetual today' as St Augustine proposed, it is pointless to wait for tomorrow. If it is 'a perpetual present', as he also suggested, then it is the present itself: it is not the converse of time, but its reality, which is to be constantly present, constantly existent, constantly in existence. 'We sense and experience that we are eternal,' writes Spinoza in the *Ethics*. This does not mean that we do not die, nor that we are not in time; what it means is that death will take nothing from us (since it will take only the future – which does not exist), that time takes nothing from us (since the present is all), lastly, that it is absurd to hope for eternity – since we are already there. 'If by eternity,' Wittgenstein said, 'is understood not endless temporal duration but timelessness, then he lives eternally who lives in the present.' In which case each of us has it, always: we are already saved. Because we are timeless? It's not the word I would use. But because, in truth, eternity is nothing more than the ever-presence of reality and truth. Who has ever lived a *yesterday* or a *tomorrow*? We live only in *todays*, and that is what we call living.

Relativity does not change this. Since Einstein, we know that time is dependent on velocity and matter, but that does not give rise to a single moment which no longer is, or one which does not yet exist. 'What Einstein's concept of relativity affects,' remarks Bachelard, 'is the period of time, the duration of time.' But not the present itself. This bears out the famous example of the Langevin twins. This is a thought experiment, but one which has been confirmed by calculation and experimentation with elementary particles. There are twin brothers, one of whom stays on earth, the other travels through space at close to the speed of light. When the latter returns, the brothers are no longer the same age: the astronaut has aged only a few months, the homebody has aged several years . . . The conclusion, doubtless accurate, is that time varies according to velocity, that there is no absolute, universal time, as Newton believed, but a series of relative or elastic times which are susceptible to expand or contract relative to velocity . . . Hence the actual. But this does not bring the past or the future into existence. Neither of the twins will have left the present for an instant. As Bachelard continues, 'the present, according to Einstein's theory, remains an absolute'. It is a point in space-time: '*hic et nunc*; not here and tomorrow, not there and today, but *here and now*'. This is the present – or rather presents, plural. Each different, shifting, but all equally present. This is what we call the universe, which does not favour either time or space: because it is space-time, and its unique incarnation.

How could we escape the present, since it is all? Why would we wish to, since the mind itself is of the present? This chapter is coming to an end, most of it is behind you now, like a past that is already fading. But you read it – can only ever read it – in the present, just as I wrote it in the present. The same is true of your life, and this is an important point. Your life is not lying in wait in the future like a wild animal or some ominous destiny. Nor is it hidden in the heavens, like a paradise or a promise. Nor is it shut up in the cave or the prison of your past. It is here and now: it is what you live and what you do. At the heart of being; at the heart of the present; at the heart of everything – in the great current of life, of reality. Nothing is set in stone; nothing is promised. If only the present exists – as the Stoics claim – only actions are real. What of dreams, imaginings, fantasies? These too are actions, because they are life, but at its lowest ebb. You would be wrong to deprive yourself of them, but wrong too to content yourself with them alone. Rather take your life in your hands: be present in the present! 'The greatest obstacle to living,' according to Seneca, 'is waiting. Everything that will happen belongs to the domain of the uncertain: live now.'

Carpe diem – seize the day? That is not enough, since the days pass, none remains. Rather seize the present, which changes and persists: *Carpe aeternitatem*.

It would be impossible to live in the moment. How could we prepare for exams, plan holidays, keep promises, live a friendship or a passion in the moment. The only option is to live in the present. How could we work, enjoy ourselves, act or love in the future?

The present is the only realm for action, for thought, for memory and for anticipation. It is the *kairos* (the right moment, the opportune moment: the moment of action) of the world, or the world as *kairos* – the real in action.

Being does not persist because it is within time; it is because being persists that time exists.

To live in the present is simply to live in reality. We are already in the Kingdom: eternity is now.

11: *Humanity*

'Man is something sacred to man'

Seneca

What is Man? This history of philosophy affords no
shortage of answers. Is Man a political animal, as
Aristotle would have it, or an animal that talks, as he
also suggested? Is he a featherless biped, as Plato
jokingly suggested? A rational animal, as the Stoics and
the Scholastics believed? Is he an animal that laughs
(Rabelais), thinks (Descartes), judges (Kant), labours
(Marx), creates (Bergson)?

None of these answers – nor indeed all of them
together – seem to me entirely satisfactory. Firstly,
because their scope is on occasion too wide; always too
narrow. A good definition should entirely circumscribe
what it defines, and it alone. This is not the case with the
famous definitions I have just cited. Imagine we could

prove that dolphins – or some extraterrestrial life form – possessed language, a political system, thought, labour, etc. This would not make either the dolphin or the alien a man any more than it would make man a cetacean or a Martian. And what of angels and their laughter?

These definitions are too broad, in that they do not apply *only* to what is defined: a person could live in society, speak, think, judge, laugh and labour . . . without being a part of humanity.

But these same definitions are also too restrictive, since they do not *wholly* circumscribe what is defined: someone who is profoundly mentally handicapped may not talk, reason, laugh, judge or take part in politics . . . He is no less *human* for all that. It can hardly be said that he lives in society any more (and perhaps less) than domestic animals. No one, however, would suggest that we treat him like an animal – however well cared for. Who would suggest that we put him in a zoo? It might be said that we have done worse things, and this is true. But what philosopher would consider such things acceptable?

If a dolphin or an alien, regardless of its intelligence, is not human and yet someone who is profoundly handicapped is (it is the latter point which is important), we must conclude that our functional or normative definitions are at fault: a human is still a human even when he has ceased to *function* normally. In other words, neither functions nor norms are sufficient definition. Humanity is not defined by what it does or what it can do. Is it defined by what it is? Almost certainly, but what is it? Neither reason, politics, laughter or labour, nor any single faculty is exclusive to man. Nothing is exclusive to man, or rather, nothing which is exclusive to him is sufficient to define him.

This is something that Diderot realized. In the entry on 'Man' in the *Encyclopédie*, he attempts a definition: 'A feeling, thinking being that moves about freely on the surface of the earth, that appears to be at the head of all animals which he dominates, that lives in society, that invented the sciences and the arts, that has a goodness and a badness particular to it, that has given itself masters, made itself laws, etc.' This definition has the same strengths and weaknesses as those we began with. But Diderot know this. And he concludes the definition with a smile that both illuminates and repudiates it: 'This word has a precise meaning only inasmuch as it reminds us of all that we are; but all that we are cannot be contained in a definition.'

Yet how can we talk about human rights unless we know what – or whom – we are dealing with? We need at least a criterion, some distinctive sign, a mark of belonging, what Aristotle would call a species difference. What is that? It is the species to which we belong. Humanity is not first and foremost a performance judged by its successes. It is a given, which can be recognized even in its failures.

This is where we must trust to biology. Not in order to discover additional distinguishing traits which would be just as debatable: upright stance, the opposable thumb, the weight of the brain, the capability to interbreed are not without their exceptions in man. If we come down to biology, it is not in order to define a concept, but to return to experience, to that of the sexual human, of conception, gestation, birth – of the body. All are born of woman: all begotten not created – the fool and the genius, the honest man and the crook, the old man as surely as the child. And this is a claim which no alien, no angel can ever make. Mankind is first and foremost a particular species of animal. We would be wrong to regret this: not only because of the keen pleasure it affords us, but because to do so would be to regret that which makes it possible for us to exist. We are mammals, Edgar Morin reminds us, we are 'of the order of primates, of the family of hominids, of the genus homo, of the species sapiens . . .' This belonging leads us to another definition, which is not functional but generic. It is the one which I fashioned for my own personal use, and which has always been sufficient: *A human being is any creature born of two human beings.* Strict biology, and cautious. Whether or not he speaks, thinks, creates, works or is capable of socialization, every creature which conforms to this definition has the same rights as we do (even if he cannot exercise those rights), or rather – though it comes to much the same thing – we have the same duties towards him.

Humanity is primarily a fact rather than a value, a species rather than a virtue. And if it can become a value or a virtue (in the sense in which humanity is the opposite of inhumanity), it is only by first being faithful to this fact, this species. 'Every man,' wrote Montaigne, 'carries within him the entire Form of human condition.' The worst among us cannot escape it. Some men are inhuman, cruel, savage, barbarous. But to contest their humanity would be to be as bad as they are. One is born a man; one becomes human. But those who fail to do so are men for all that. Humanity is a given, before it is created or creative. Natural before being cultural. It is not an essence, it is a descent: man, because son of man.

This raises the problems of cloning, of eugenics, of the eventual artificial fabrication of man – or of superman. And, to me, it is a compelling reason to reject them. If humanity defines itself by filiation rather than by its essence, through birth rather than through mind, by the duties it owes to others rather than its functions or performance, then we must hold to that filiation, to that birth, to those duties. Humanity is not a game, it is an issue. Not primarily a creation, but a legacy. Not an invention but an allegiance. Nobody would think of protesting against the remarkable progress in genetics being used to restore to every human being his full humanity (what we call gene therapy). But this is not a reason to seek to transform humanity itself, even to improve on it. Medicine fights illness; but humanity is not an illness: therefore it does not legitimately fall under the domain of medicine.

To improve on man would be to betray or to lose him.

All beings tend to persevere in their essence, said Spinoza, and the essence of man would no less be destroyed by his becoming an angel than by his becoming a horse . . . Eugenics and barbarism on the same side! Certainly, we should heal the individual; we can never do enough, but we should not modify the human species. I realize that in gene therapy the line between the two is tenuous, even problematic. All the more reason to reflect on it and to be vigilant. Man is not God: he can remain truly human only on condition that he accepts that he is neither its cause nor its ruin.

If humanity is above all a species of animal, this raises the important matter of humanism. The word can be interpreted in two ways. There is practical or moral humanism, which simply accords a certain value to humanity – in other words, imposing on oneself a certain number of duties and proscriptions as regards our behaviour to others. Nowadays, we refer to these as human rights, or rather the philosophical foundation of human rights: we can have such rights chiefly because we all have duties to one another. Not to kill, torture, oppress, enslave, rape, steal, humiliate, slander . . . Such humanism is more a moral than a political stance, and, for the most part, it is one shared by our contemporaries. Why do we no longer consider masturbation or homo-sexuality to be wrong? Because they harm no one. Why do we condemn rape, pimping, paedophilia more passionately than ever? Because such behaviour entails or threatens violence, it enslaves, exploits or oppresses others, in short because it infringes on the human rights of another, his integrity, his freedom, his dignity . . . This says a lot about how morality has changed in secular societies. It is no longer a submission to absolute or transcendent commandments, but derives from a consideration for the welfare of humanity, for this individual man, that woman. It is no longer an adjunct to religion, but the essence of practical humanism. Why 'practical'? Because it concerns action (*praxis*) rather than thought or contemplation (*theoria*). It is not about what we know or believe humanity to be, but what we want it to be. If man is sacred to man, as Seneca suggests, it is not because he is a God, nor because a God commands him. It is because he is Man, and that is enough.

Practical humanism: humanism as morality, humane action for the benefit of humanity.

But there is another form, which may be called theoretical or transcendental humanism. What is it? It is a certain way of thinking, a certain belief, a certain knowledge, or at least presents itself as such: it encompasses what we should know of man and his worth, or what we should believe in order to provide the foundation for our duties towards him . . . This form of humanism stumbles on the very knowledge it purports to possess. For what we know of man is that he is more often capable of the worst – consider Auschwitz – and the mediocre than he is of the best. Secondly – consider Darwin – that he has not chosen to be what he is (he is a product rather than a principle). Lastly, that he is not God, since he has a body (which prevents him from being either all-powerful or immortal); a history, first natural, then cultural; and finally a society and a subconscious which govern him far more, alas, than he governs them. It is here that the human sciences – Freud, Marx, Durkheim – overthrow the idea that we are capable of creating ourselves: their theoretical anti-humanism, as Althusser put it, prevents us from believing in Man as we once believed in God, or, in other words, of making him the basis of his being, his thoughts and his actions. 'The ultimate goal of the human sciences,' writes Lévi-Strauss, 'is not to create man but to dissolve him', which supposes reintegrating 'culture into nature, and eventually, life into the ensemble of its physio-chemical components'. Man is not his own cause, nor is he, for the most part, master of himself, still less transparent to himself. He is the result of a particular history which, unbeknownst to him, runs through him and constitutes him. He is what he does only because of what has made him who he is (his body, his past, his education . . .). If Man is, as Sartre claims, 'condemned at every moment to invent man', he does not do so out of nothing. Humanity is not a blank page, nor a pure creation of the self by the self. It is a history; an inevitability; it is an adventure.

'Man is not an empire within an empire,' Spinoza wrote: he is a part of nature, whose laws he follows (even when he appears to violate or vandalize them); he is a part of history, which he shapes and which shapes him; he is a part of a society, an age, a civilization . . . That he is capable of the worst is only too easy to explain. He is an animal destined to die; an animal aware of his mortality; an animal with urges rather than instincts, passions rather than reason, fantasies rather than thoughts, anger rather than wisdom. Edgar Morin has a charming expression: '*Homo sapiens, homo demens*'. Mankind is so full of violence, of desire, of fear! We are right to protect ourselves from him, it is the only way to deal with him.

'I lament the fate of humanity,' wrote La Mettrie, 'that it is, so to speak, entrusted to hands as despicable as its own.' But there are no others: our solitude dictates our duties. What the human sciences teach us about ourselves is precious, but it could not take the place of morality. What we *know* of man says nothing – or very little – about what we *would wish* him to be. The fact that selfishness, violence or cruelty can be scientifically explained (why should they not be, since they exist), tells us little about Man's worth. Love, gentleness and compassion can also be explained – they too exist and are more worthy. In whose name? In the name of a certain idea of man according to Spinoza, 'as an exemplar of human nature towards which we may look'. To understand is not to judge, nor does it make judging any less necessary. The theoretical anti-humanism of the human sciences, far from devaluing practical humanism, is what confers on it its importance and its status. It is not a religion, but a morality; not a theory but a struggle. It is the struggle for human rights, and it is the chief duty of each of us.

Humanity is not an essence to be contemplated, nor an absolute to be revered, nor a God to be adored: it is a species to be preserved, a history to be known, a group of individuals to be acknowledged, lastly a value to be defended. It is, as I said of morality, a case of not being unworthy of what humanity has made of itself and of us. This is what I call faithfulness, something which is more important to me than faith.

Should we believe in man? Better to know him as he is and beware of him. But this should not exempt us from keeping faith with the best that men and women have achieved – civilization, intelligence, humanity itself – what is handed down to us, what we wish to pass on, in short, with a certain idea of man but one which owes less to knowing than to recognizing, less to the sciences than to the *humanities*, as they used to be called, less to religion than to morality and history. Practical rather than theoretical humanism: the only humanism worth the name is humane action.

At the end of his *Apology of Raymond Sebond*, Montaigne recalls a phrase from Seneca: 'O, what a vile and abject thing is Man if he does not rise above humanity!', and adds this commentary: 'A pithy saying, a most useful aspiration, but absurd withal. For to make a fistful bigger than the fist, an armful larger than the arm, or to try and make your stride wider than your legs can stretch, are things monstrous and impossible. Nor may a man mount above himself or above humanity.' All that remains – and there is no guarantee of this – is for him not to sink beneath it.

All that remains is humanism without illusions to safeguard it. Man is not dead: neither as a species, nor as an ideal. But he is mortal, and that is one more reason to fight for him.

12: *Wisdom*

'Learned we may be with another man's learning: we
can only be wise with wisdom of our own'

Montaigne

The etymology is straightforward: *philosophia*, in Greek,
is the love of – or the search for – wisdom. But what is
wisdom? Is it knowledge? Certainly this is the usual
meaning of the word – *sophia* in Greek, *sapientia* in Latin
– as confirmed by most philosophers since Heraclitus.
For Plato as for Spinoza, for the Stoics as for Descartes
and Kant, for Epicurus as for Montaigne or Alain,
wisdom has much to do with thought, with intelligence
and with learning; it is, therefore, a kind of *knowledge*.
But a very specific kind, which no science can confirm,
no proof substantiate, which no laboratory can test or
attest and which cannot be conferred by any diploma.
Wisdom is practical rather than theoretical, it deals not

in proofs but in tests, not in experiment but in action, not in science but in life.

The Greeks sometimes distinguished between theoretical or contemplative wisdom (*sophia*) and practical wisdom (*phronesis*). But one cannot exist without the other and true wisdom would be a synthesis of the two. In French we barely distinguish between them. 'Judge well in order to act well,' as Descartes rightly put it. Clearly some people are more capable of contemplation and others of action. But no single gift can confer wisdom: some may have to learn to judge, others to act. Neither intelligence, nor culture, nor skill is sufficient in itself. 'Wisdom cannot be a science nor a skill,' Aristotle emphasized: it is less about what is true or efficient and more about what is good for oneself and for others. It is a kind of knowledge – the knowledge of how to live.

This is what distinguishes wisdom from philosophy, which is the knowledge of how to think. But philosophy has meaning only if it brings us closer to wisdom: the only true philosophy is that which helps us to think better in order to live better. 'Philosophy is the art which teaches us how to live,' writes Montaigne. Does this mean that we don't know how to live? Of course: it is because we are not wise that we need philosophy. Wisdom is the goal, philosophy the path.

I'm reminded of a line from Aragon: 'Time to learn how to live, it is already too late . . .' Montaigne says something similar ('They teach us to live when our life is over'), though he is more optimistic, seeing this less as a fatal flaw in the human condition than a fault of education which can and should be corrected. Why wait to philosophize when life does not wait? 'A hundred students have got the pox before they have come to read Aristotle's lecture on temperance . . .' What does the pox have to do with philosophy? Nothing, as far as treatment or prevention goes. But getting the pox concerns sexuality, prudence and pleasure, love and death . . . How could medicine or prophylaxis be sufficient in themselves? How could they take the place of wisdom? 'You are not dying because you are ill,' Montaigne writes elsewhere in the *Essays*; 'you are dying because you are alive.' We must therefore learn to die, learn to live, that is what philosophy means. 'It is a great mistake,' Montaigne continues, 'to portray Philosophy with a haughty, frowning, terrifying face, or as inaccessible to the young. Whoever clapped that wan and frightening mask on her face! There is nothing more lovely, more happy and gay – I almost said more amorously playful.' Too bad for those who confuse philosophy with erudition, discipline with boredom, wisdom with dusty books. The very fact that life is as difficult, as fragile, as dangerous and as precious as it undoubtedly is is all the more reason to begin philosophy as early as possible ('children need to learn it as much as we do at other ages'), in other words, to learn how to live, while we still can, *before* it is too late.

This is the purpose of philosophy and the reason why it is appropriate to all ages, at least as soon as one has begun to master thought and language. Why should children who study maths, physics, history, music, not study philosophy? All the more so those who are studying to become doctors or engineers? And when do adults, overwhelmed with work and worries, find the time to begin or to continue to study it? Of course we have to earn a living; but that does not exempt us from living. How can we live intelligently without taking the time to think about life, by ourselves or with others, without questioning, without reasoning, without discussing life in the most radical and rigorous way possible, without concerning ourselves with what others who are more knowledgeable or more talented than the average thought about it? When discussing art, I quoted Malraux: 'It is in museums that we learn to paint.' I would contend that it is in books of philosophy that we learn how to philosophize. But the goal is not philosophy itself, still less the books. The goal is a happier, freer, simpler – wiser – life. Which of us could claim that his life could not be better? In 'On the education of children' (*Essays*, I, 26) Montaigne cites the same line from Horace that Kant will later make the maxim of the Enlightenment: '*Sapere aude, incipe*: dare to know – dare to be wise – begin!' Why wait any longer? Why put off happiness? It is never too early nor too late to philosophize, to paraphrase Epicurus, since it is never too early nor too late to be happy. So be it. But by the same logic, the earlier the better.

*

But what kind of wisdom? On this as on everything, philosophers disagree. The wisdom of pleasure proposed by Epicurus: the Stoics' wisdom of the will; the Sceptics' wisdom of silence; Spinoza's wisdom of knowledge and love; Kant's of duty and hope? We must each form our own opinion on the subject, which may borrow from several different schools of thought. This is why each person must philosophize for himself: because no one can think or live in your stead. But what all – or almost all – philosophers agree on is the sense of happiness, of serenity, which characterizes wisdom, it is a joyful yet lucid inner peace which accompanies the rigorous use of reason. It is the antithesis of anxiety, of madness, of unhappiness. This is why wisdom is necessary. This is why we must philosophize. Because we do not know how to live. Because we must learn. Because we are constantly threatened by anxiety, madness and unhappiness.

'The evil most contrary to wisdom,' writes Alain, 'is foolishness.' This also tells us what we should strive towards: towards the most *intelligent* life possible. But intelligence in itself is not enough; books are not enough. What is the point of thinking so much if one lives so little? How much knowledge is there in the sciences, in economics, in philosophy? And yet how much foolishness in the lives of scientists, businessmen and philosophers? Intelligence nurtures wisdom insofar as it transforms, or illuminates, or guides our lives. It is not enough to invent systems, to use concepts, or rather, concepts are merely a means to an end. The only goal is to think and to live a little better, or a little less badly.

Marcus Aurelius puts it well: 'If the gods took counsel together about myself, and what should befall me, then their counsel was good . . . Yet even if it is true that they care nothing for our mortal concerns, I am still able to take care of myself and to look to my own interests . . .' Wisdom is not saintliness. Philosophy is neither a religion nor a moral system. It is my life I am trying to save, not the lives of others; my own interests I am fighting for, not those of God or of humanity. That, at least, is my starting point. It is possible that I shall encounter God along the way; probable that I shall encounter humanity. But even then I shall not renounce the life given to me, my freedom, my clarity of mind, nor my happiness.

How should we live? That is the question which philosophy has sought to tackle since its inception. The answer is wisdom, but wisdom made flesh, brought to life, put into action: it is up to each of us to create our own. This is where ethics – the art of living – distinguishes itself from morality, which concerns only our duties. That they can and should work in harmony is obvious. To ask how we should live is also to ask what role our duties should play. Nonetheless, the aims are very different. Morality answers the question: 'What should I do?'; ethics, the question: 'How should I live?' The apotheosis of morality is virtue or saintliness; that of ethics, wisdom or happiness. Thou shalt not kill, steal, lie? Certainly, but would that be enough for anyone? Who would consider it happiness enough, freedom enough, salvation enough? A friend once said to me: 'Not catching AIDS is not enough of a goal in life.' He was right, obviously. But neither is not killing, not stealing, not lying. No 'thou shalt not' can be sufficient, this is why we need wisdom: because morality is not enough, because duty is not enough, because virtue is not enough. Morality commands, but who would be happy merely to obey? Morality says 'no', but who would be happy only with proscriptions? Love is more precious. Knowledge is more precious. Freedom is more precious. We must say 'yes': yes to ourselves, yes to others, yes to the world, yes to everything: that is the meaning of wisdom. *'Amor fati,'* writes Nietzsche, alluding to the Stoics: 'that one wants nothing to be other than it is, not in the future, not in the past, not in all eternity . . . *love.'*

This does not preclude revolt, nor does it preclude struggle. To say yes to the world is to say yes to our own revolt, which is a part of it; to our actions, which are a part of it. Consider Albert Camus or Cavaillès. To transform the real is to suppose that we accept it as it is. To bring about something that does not yet exist pre-supposes working with what is. No one can do otherwise. Wisdom is not a utopia. No utopia is wise. The world is not to be dreamed but to be transformed. Wisdom is, first and foremost, a certain relationship with truth and with action, an invigorating lucidity; it is knowledge which is active, in action. To see things as they are, to know what one wants. Not to delude oneself, not to pretend. 'Not to play the tragic actor,' says Marcus Aurelius. To know and to accept. To understand and to transform. To resist and to overcome. For it is impossible to confront anything unless one accepts its existence. It is impossible to be healed unless we accept illness; impossible to fight injustice if we do not acknowledge it. We must accept reality as it is, for we cannot transform what we do not accept.

This is the approach of Stoicism: to accept those things for which we are not responsible; to act on those things for which we are. It is Spinoza's approach: know, understand, act. It is also that of the sages of the Orient, Prajnânpad, for example: 'See and accept that which is and then, if needs be, try to change it.' The wise man acts where generally we simply hope and tremble. He confronts what is, where habitually all we can do is hope for that which is not yet or regret that which is no longer. Prajnânpad again: 'What is done has become the past; it does not exist now. What will happen is in the future and does not exist now. So? What exists? What is here and now. Nothing more . . . Stay in the present: act, act, act!' Wisdom is living your life rather than hoping to live, and creating your own salvation as far as is possible, rather than waiting for it.

Wisdom brings together the greatest possible happiness with the greatest possible lucidity. It is the good life, as the Greeks said, but a life which is humane; one which is responsible and dignified. Enjoy it, rejoice in it as much as possible. But not anyhow and not at any price. 'Everything which brings joy is good,' writes Spinoza; 'but not all joys are of equal worth.' 'Every pleasure is good,' writes Epicurus. That does not mean that all are worth seeking out, nor even that all are acceptable. We must choose, therefore, weigh the advantages and disadvantages, as Epicurus also said; in, other words we must judge. This is the purpose of wisdom. By the same token it is also the purpose of philosophy. One does not philosophize to pass the time, nor to be noticed, nor to tinker with ideas: one does so to save one's skin and one's soul.

Wisdom is that salvation, not in some other life, but in this one. Is it something we can attain? Probably not entirely. But that is not a reason not to try to move towards it. No one is absolutely wise; but who would resign himself to being completely mad?

If you wish to advance, said the Stoics, you must know where you are headed. Wisdom is the goal: life is the goal, but a life that is happier and more lucid; happiness is the goal, but one which is lived in the truth.

Be careful, however, not to make wisdom into another ideal, another hope, another utopia; to do so would be to cut yourself off from the real. Wisdom is not another life for which we should wait, towards which we should strive. It is this life lived in the truth which we must know and love. Because it is loveable? Not necessarily, nor always. But so that it might become so.

'The most express sign of wisdom,' says Montaigne, 'is unruffled joy; like all in the realms above the moon, her state is ever serene.' I could also quote Socrates, Epicurus ('one must laugh as one philosophizes'), Descartes, Spinoza, Diderot or Alain . . . All of them have argued that wisdom is on the side of pleasure, of joy, of action, of love. And that chance is not enough.

It is not because the wise man is happier than we that he loves life more. It is because he loves life more that he is happier.

As for us, who are not wise, who are mere apprentices of wisdom – philosophers, in other words – we must learn how to live, learn how to think, learn how to love. The task will never be completed, which is why we will always need to philosophize.

It is not without its struggles, but neither is it without its joys. 'In all other occupations,' writes Epicurus, 'joy follows a task completed with difficulty; but in philosophy, pleasure walks side by side with knowledge: it is not after one has learned that one rejoices in what one knows; learning and rejoicing go hand in hand.'

Take heart: truth is not at the end of the road; it is the road itself.

Bibliography

In this short book, which is intended merely as an introduction, it seemed to me preferable to avoid footnotes which would inevitably have been copious and would have needlessly weighed down the whole. The following bibliography indicates, chapter by chapter, most of the books I have cited or alluded to, or which seem to me important propitious to more considered reflection: it is less a list of references than a suggested reading list. The editions mentioned are indicative (where possible, I have favoured those in paperback). Lastly, I have put an asterisk against those works which are most accessible, those which I believe might most profitably be read first; two asterisks against those which are moderately difficult, three asterisks denote the most difficult works which would be best saved until last. Obviously, this does not indicate a hierarchy of the quality of these works. Some masterpieces are effortless, others dauntingly abstruse – and there are many abstruse books (which are not found on this list) which are far from being masterpieces . . . In any case, there are no philosophical books which do not demand some effort of the reader. This does not mean that reading them is not a pleasure, but that, in philosophy, pleasure and effort go hand in hand.

Introduction

Plato, *The Last Days of Socrates**, trans. Hugh Tredennick (Penguin Classics)

Epicurus, *Letters and Maxims***, from *Essential Epicurus*, trans. Eugene O'Connor (Prometheus Books)

Marcus Aurelius, *Meditations**, trans. Maxwell Staniforth (Penguin Classics)

Michel de Montaigne, *The Complete Essays***, trans. M. A. Screech (Penguin Classics)

René Descartes, *Discouse on Method and The Meditations**, trans. F. E. Sutcliffe (Penguin Classics)

Blaise Pascal, *Pensées**, trans. A. J. Krailsheimer (Penguin Classics)

Benedict Spinoza, *On the Improvement of Understanding***, trans. R. H. M. Elwes (Dover)

Immanuel Kant, *Opus posthumus****, trans. Eckart Förster and Michael Rosen (Cambridge University Press)

G. W. F. Hegel, *Phenomenology of Spirit****, trans. A. V. Miller (Oxford University Press)

Friedrich Nietzsche, *The Gay Science***, trans. Adrian del Caro (Cambridge University Press)

Gilles Deleuze, *What is Philosophy?****, trans. Felix Guattari, Graham Birchill and Hugh Tomlinson (Verso Books)

Pierre Hadot, *What is Ancient Philosophy?***, trans. Michael Chase (The Belknap Press)

1. Morality

Plato, *The Republic***, trans. Desmond Lee (Penguin Classics)

Epictetus, *The Discourses of Epictetus*** (Everyman Series Phoenix)

Benedict Spinoza, *Ethics****, trans. G. H. R. Parkinson (Oxford University Press)

Jean-Jacques Rousseau, *A Discourse on Inequality**, trans. Maurice Cranston (Penguin Classics)

David Hume, *Enquiries Concerning Human Understanding and Concerning the Principles of Morals*** (Oxford University Press)

Immanuel Kant, *Groundwork for the Metaphysics of Morals***, trans. Arnulf Zweig (Oxford University Press). On the relationship between religion and morality, see also *Religion within the Boundaries of Mere Reason*, trans. George Di Giovanni (Cambridge University Press)

Arthur Schopenhauer, *On the Basis of Morality***, trans. E. F. J. Payne (Hackett)

John Stuart Mill, *Utilitarianism***, ed. Roger Crisp (Oxford University Press)

Friedrich Nietzsche, *The Genealogy of Morals*** (Dover Publications)

Ludwig Wittgenstein, *Philosophical Investigations***, trans. G. E. M. Anscombe (Blackwell)

Michel Foucault, *The History of Sexuality: The Care of the Self***, trans. Robert Hurley (Penguin Books)

Emmanuel Lévinas, *Ethics and Infinity*** (Duquesne University Press)

Hans Jonas, *The Imperative of Responsibility: In Search of an Ethic for the Technological Age*** (University of Chicago Press)

Paul Ricoeur, *Oneself as Another****, trans. Kathleen Blamey (University of Chicago Press)

André Comte-Sponville, *A Short Treatise on the Great Virtues**, trans. Frank Wynne (Vintage)

2. Politics

Plato, *The Republic***, trans. Desmond Lee (Penguin Classics)

Aristotle, *The Politics***, trans. Sir Ernest Barker (Oxford University Press)

Niccoló Machiavelli, *The Prince**, trans. P. Bondella and Mark Musa (Oxford University Press)

Estienne De La Boétie, *The Politics of Obedience: The Discourse of Voluntary Servitude** (Black Rose Books)

Michel de Montaigne, *The Complete Essays***, trans. M. A. Screech (Penguin Classics)

Thomas Hobbes, *Leviathan*** (Oxford University Press)

Blaise Pascal, *Pensées**, trans. A. J. Krailsheimer (Penguin Classics)

Benedict Spinoza, *Political Treatise***, trans. Samuel Shirley (Hackett)

John Locke, *Two Treatises of Government*** (Cambridge University Press)

Montesquieu (Charles Louis de Secondat), *Spirits of the Laws*** (Prometheus Books)

Jean-Jacques Rousseau, *The Social Contract***, trans. Maurice Cranston (Penguin Classics)

G. W. F. Hegel, *Philosophy of Right****, trans. T. M. Knox (Oxford University Press)

Benjamin Constant, *Political Writings*** (Cambridge University Press)

Alexis de Toqueville, *Democracy in America***, trans. Gerald Bevan (Penguin Classics)

Karl Marx and Friedrich Engels, *The Communist Manifesto** (Oxford University Press)

John Rawls, *A Theory of Justice*** (Oxford University Press)

Albert Camus, *The Rebel**, trans. Anthony Bower (Penguin Books)

Regis Debray, *Critique of Political Reason*** (Verso). On the differences between republic and democracy, see also the first essay in *Contretemps,* 'Eloges des idéaux perdus' (Gallimard)

Karl Popper, *The Open Society and Its Enemies*** (Routledge)

3. Love

Plato, 'The banquet'* from *Symposium* (Oxford University Press)

Aristotle, *The Nicomachean Ethics***, trans. J. A. K. Thompson (Penguin Classics); see also *Eudemian Ethics* (Oxford University Press) and *The Art of Rhetoric*, trans. Hugh Lawson-Tancred (Penguin Classics)

Michel de Montaigne, *The Complete Essays*** (in particular 'On affectionate relationships'), trans. M. A. Scrrech (Penguin Classics)

René Descartes, *The Passions of the Soul***, trans. Stephen Voss (Hackett)

Benedict Spinoza, *Ethics****, trans. G. H. R. Parkinson (Oxford University Press)

Arthur Schopenhauer, *Metaphysics of Love***, from Volume IV of *The World as Will and Representation*, trans. E. F. J. Payne (Dover)

George Simmel, *The Philosophy of Love***

Alain (Émile-Auguste Chartier), 'Les Sentiments familiaux'**, from
   Les Passions et la sagesse (Gallimard)
Simone Weil, *Gravity and Grace** (Routledge Classics)
Denis De Rougemont, *Love in the Western World**, trans.
   Montgomery Belgion (Princeton University Press)
Vladimir Jankelevitch, *Les Vertus de l'amour*** (*Traité des virtues*, II),
   (Flammarion)
André Comte-Sponville, *L'Amour la solitude**, (Albin Michel); see
   also Chapter 18 of *A Short Treatise on the Great Virtues**, trans.
   Frank Wynne (Vintage)
Marcel Conche, *Analyse de l'amour et autres sujets*** (Presses
   universitaires de France); see also *Le Sens de la philosophie***
   (Encre Marine)

4. Death

Plato, *Phaedo**, ed. David Gallop (Oxford University Press)
Epicurus, *Letters and Maxims**, from *Essential Epicurus*, trans.
   Eugene O'Connor (Prometheus Books)
Lucretius (Titus Lucretius Carus), *On the Nature of the Universe***,
   trans. R. E. Latham (Penguin Classics)
Seneca (Lucius Annaeus Seneca), *Letters from a Stoic: Epistulae
   Morales ad Lucilium***, trans. Robin Campbell (Penguin Classics)
Marcus Aurelius, *Meditations**, trans. Maxwell Staniforth (Penguin
   Classics)
Michel de Montaigne, *The Complete Essays*** (especially 'To
   philosophize is to learn how to die' and 'On the armour of the
   Parthians'), trans. M. A. Screech (Penguin Classics)
Blaise Pascal, *Pensées**, trans. A. J. Krailsheimer (Penguin Books)
Sigmund Freud, 'Beyond the Pleasure Principle', from *On
   Metapsychology – The Theory of Psychoanalysis and Other Works***
   (Penguin Freud Library)
Vladimir Jankelevitch, *La Mort*** (Flammarion)
Marcel Conche, *La Mort et la pensée***, from *Orientation
   philosophique*** (Presses universitaires de France)
Françoise Dastur, *Death: An Essay on Finitude*** trans. John
   Llewelyn (Continuum International/Athlone)
Vincent Cordonnier, *La Mort** (Quintette)

5. Knowledge

Plato, *The Republic***, trans. Desmond Lee (Penguin Classics)

Michel de Montaigne, 'An apology for Raymond Sebond', from *The Complete Essays***, trans. M. A. Screech (Penguin Classics)

René Descartes, *Discourse on Method and The Meditations**, trans. F. E. Sutcliffe (Penguin Classics)

Blaise Pascal, *On the Geometrical Mind**

Benedict Spinoza, *On the Improvement of Understanding***, trans. R. H. M. Elwes (Dover)

John Locke, *An Essay Concerning Human Understanding*** (Everyman)

Gottfried Leibniz, *New Essays on Human Understanding*** (Cambridge University Press)

David Hume, *Enquiries Concerning Human Understanding and Concerning the Principles of Morals*** (Oxford University Press). This is his most accessible work, though his masterpiece is *A Treatise of Human Nature*** (Oxford University Press)

Immanuel Kant, *Critique of Pure Reason****, trans. Paul Guyer and Allen W. Wood (Cambridge University Press); see also 'An answer to the question: What is enlightenment?', in *Practical Philosophy***, trans. Mary J. Gregor (Cambridge University Press)

Friedrich Nietzsche, *The Gay Science**, trans. Adrian del Caro (Cambridge University Press)

Martin Heidegger, *The Essence of Truth: On Plato's 'Parable of the Cave' and the 'Theaetetus'***, trans. Ted Sadler (Continuum International/Athlone)

Alain (Émile-Auguste Chartier), *Entretiens au bord de la mer** (Gallimard)

Gaston Bachelard, *Formation of the Scientific Spirit*** (Philosophy of Science Series, Clinamen)

Karl Popper, *The Logic of Scientific Discovery*** (Routledge Classics)

André Comte-Sponville, *Valeur et vérite*** (Presses universitaires de France)

Francis Wolff, *Dire le Monde**** (Presses universitaires de France)

Pascal Engel, *Truth*** (Acumen)

Jean-Michel Besnier, *Les théories de la connaissance*** (Flammarion)

6. Liberty

Plato, *The Republic*** (the myth of Er is in Book X), trans. Desmond Lee (Penguin Classics)

Aristotle, *The Nicomachean Ethics***, trans. J. A. K. Thompson (Penguin Classics)

Epictetus, *The Discourses of Epictetus** (Everyman Series, Phoenix)

Thomas Hobbes, *On the Citizen*** (Cambridge University Press)

René Descartes, Philosophical Letters** (Oxford University Press)

Benedict Spinoza, *Letters***, trans. Samuel Shirley (Hackett)

Gottfried Leibniz, *Philosophical Essays*** (Hackett)

Voltaire (François-Marie Arouet), *Philosophical Dictionary**, trans. Theodore Besterman (Penguin Classics)

Immanuel Kant, *Critique of Practical Reason****, trans. Paul Guyer and Allen M. Wood (Cambridge University Press)

Arthur Schopenhauer, 'Essay on free will'**, from *Essays and Aphorisms* (Penguin Classics)

Henri Bergson, *Time and Free Will: Essay on the Immediate Data of Consciousness*** (R. A. Kessinger)

Alain (Émile-Auguste Chartier), 'Histoire de mes pensées'*, from *Les Arts et les dieux* (Gallimard)

Jean-Paul Sartre, 'Cartesian freedom'**, from *Essays in Existentialism*** (Citadel Press); see also 'Existentialism is a humanism'* and most importantly *Being and Nothingness****, trans. Hazel E. Barnes (Routledge)

Marcel Conche, *L'aléatoire*** (Presses universitaires de France)

Karl Popper 'The open universe: An argument for indeterminism'**, from *Postscript to the Logic of Scientific Discovery*, ed. William Warren Barftley (Hutchinson Educational)

7. God

Aristotle, *The Metaphysics****, trans. Hugh Lawson-Tancred (Penguin Classics)

René Descartes, *Meditations and Other Metaphysical Writings** (Addison Wesley)

Benedict Spinoza, *Ethics****, trans. G. H. R. Parkinson (Oxford University Press)

Blaise Pascal, *Pensées**, trans. A. J. Krailsheimer (Penguin Classics)

Nicolas Malebranche, *Dialogues on Metaphysics and on Religion*** (Cambridge University Press)

Gottfried Wilhelm Leibniz, *Discourse on Metaphysics and Other Essays: Discourse on Metaphysics; On the Ultimate Origination of Things; Preface to the New Essays; The Monadology**** (Hackett)

David Hume, *Dialogues Concerning Natural Religion*** (Oxford

World's Classics)

Jean-Jacques Rousseau, 'Profession of faith of a Savoyard vicar'*, from *Emile: Selections* (Heinemann)

Immanuel Kant, *Critique of Pure Reason****, trans. Paul Guyer and Allen W. Wood (Cambridge University Press); see also *Religion within the Boundaries of Mere Reason***, trans. George Di Giovanni (Cambridge University Press)

Soren Kierkegaard, *Fear and Trembling***, trans. Alastair Hannay (Penguin Classics)

Henri Bergson, *The Two Sources of Morality and Religion*** (Greenwood Press)

Alain (Émile-Auguste Chartier), *Les Dieux** (Gallimard); the closing section, 'Christophore', is the most beautiful piece on Christianity I know.

Martin Heidegger, *Identity and Difference*** (HarperCollins)

Simone Weil, *Waiting for God*** (Perennial)

Ludwig Wittgenstein, *Notebooks***, ed. G. H. von Wright (University of Chicago Press)

Lévinas, Emmanuel, *Of God Who Comes to Mind***, trans. Bettina Bergo (Stanford University Press)

Jean-Luc Marion, *God without Being: Hors-texte***, trans. Thomas A. Carlson (University of Chicago Press)

Bernard Sève, *La Question philosophique de l'existence de Dieu*** (Presses universitaires de France)

8. Atheism

Lucretius (Titus Lucretius Carus) *On the Nature of the Universe***, trans. R. E. Latham (Penguin Classics)

David Hume, *Dialogues Concerning Natural Religion*** (Oxford World's Classics)

Denis Diderot, *Entretien d'un philosophe avec la maréchale de —*** (Actes Sud)

Paul Henri Thiry d'Holbach, *Good Sense***, trans. Anna Knoop (Prometheus Books)

Ludwig Feuerbach, *The Essence of Religion*** (Prometheus Books)

Arthur Schopenhauer, *Religion: A Dialogue and Other Essays***, trans. T. B. Saunders (Greenwood Press)

Karl Marx and Friedrich Engels, *On Religion*** (Oxford University Press)

Friedrich Nietzsche, *The Gay Science***, trans. Adrian del Caro

(Cambridge University Press); see also *The Antichrist***, trans. Domino Falls (Creation Books)

Sigmund Freud, *The Future of an Illusion and Other Writings***, trans. Jim Underwood (Penguin Books)

Jean-Paul Sartre, 'Existentialism is a humanism'*, from *Essays in Existentialism* (Citadel Press)

Albert Camus, *The Myth of Sisyphus**, trans. Justin O'Brien (Penguin Books)

Marcel Conche, *Orientation philosophique*** (Presses universitaires de France)

Robert Joly, *Dieu vous interpelle? Moi, il m'évite . . .*** (Editions EPO)

9. Art

Aristotle, *Poetics*** (Penguin Classics)

Immanuel Kant, *Critique of Judgement****, trans. Werner S. Pluhar (Hackett), especially the first section

Arthur Schopenhauer, *The World as Will and Representation***, trans. E. F. J. Payne (Dover), especially Book III

G. W. F. Hegel, *Introductory Lectures on Aesthetics***, trans. R. D. Bosanquet (Penguin Classics)

F. W. J. Schelling, *The Philosophy of Art***, trans. D. W. Stott (University of Minnesota Press)

Friedrich Nietzsche, *The Birth of Tragedy***, (Oxford World's Classics)

Alain (Émile-Auguste Chartier), *Système des beaux-arts*** (Gallimard)

Martin Heidegger, 'The origin of the work of art' (1936) in *Basic Writings***, ed. D. Krell (HarperCollins)

Luc Ferry, *Homo aestheticus: L'Invention du goût à l'âge démocratique*** (Grasset)

Michel Haar, *L'Oeuvre d'art: Essai sur l'ontologie des oeuvres*** (Hatier)

Renée Bouveresse, *L'Expérience esthétique*** (Armand Colin)

10. Time

Aristotle, *Physics****, trans. Robin Waterfield (Oxford World's Classics)

Plotinus, *Ennead*** (III, 7: 'Of time and eternity'), trans. H. Armstrong (Loeb Classical Library)

St. Augustine, *Confessions**, trans. R. S. Pine-Coffin (Penguin Classics)

Immanuel Kant, *Critique of Pure Reason****, trans. Paul Guyer and Allen W. Wood (Cambridge University Press)

Bergson, Henri, *Matter and Memory***, trans. N. M. Paul and W. S. Palmer (Zone Books)

Edmund Husserl, *On the Phenomenology of the Consciousness of Internal Time***, trans. Ted Klein (Kluwer Academic)

Martin Heidegger, *Being and Time****, trans. J. Macquarrie and E. Robinson (Blackwell)

Maurice Merleau-Ponty, *Phenomenology of Perception*** (Routledge Classics)

Victor Goldschmidt, *Le Système stoïcien et l'idée de temps*** (Vrin)

Marcel Conche, *Temps et destin*** (Presses universitaires de Frances)

Marc Wetzel, *Le Temps*** (Quintette)

Nicolas Grimaldi, *Ontologie du temps*** (Presses universitaires de Frances)

André Comte-Sponville, *L'être temps*** (Presses universitaires de Frances)

11. Humanity

Michel de Montaigne, *The Complete Essays***, trans. M. A. Screech (Penguin Classics)

Blaise Pascal, *Pensées**, trans. A. J. Krailsheimer (Penguin Classics)

David Hume, *A Treatise of Human Nature**** (Oxford University Press)

Jean-Jacques Rousseau, *A Discourse on Inequality**, trans. Maurice Cranston (Penguin Classics)

Immanuel Kant, *Anthropology from a Pragmatic Point of View****, trans. Victor Lyle Dowdell (Southern Illinois University Press)

Martin Heidegger, 'Letter on humanism'**, from *Heidegger: Off the Beaten Track*** (Cambridge University Press)

Jean-Paul Sartre, 'Existentialism is a humanism'*, from *Essays in Existentialism* (Citadel Press)

Simone De Beauvoir, *The Second Sex*** (Vintage Classics)

Claude Lévi-Strauss, *Savage Mind*** (Weidenfeld and Nicolson)

Emmanuel Lévinas, *Humanism and the Other*** (Duquesne University Press)

Louis Althusser, *For Marx*** (Verso Classics)

Edgar Morin, *Le Paradigm perdu: la nature humaine*** (Seuil)

Michel Foucault, *The Order of Things: An Archaeology of the Human Sciences*** (Routledge Classics)

Jean-Michel Besnier, *L'Humanisme déchiré*** (Descartes et Cie)
Luc Ferry, *Man Made God: The Meaning of Life**, trans. David Pellauer (University of Chicago Press)
André Comte-Sponville and Luc Ferry, *La Sagesse des modernes*** (Laffont)
Tzvetan Todorov, *The Imperfect Garden: The Legacy of Humanism***, trans. Carol Cosman (Princeton University Press)
Luc Ferry and Jean-Didier Vincent, *Qu'est-ce que l'homme?*** (Odile Jacob)

12. Wisdom

Plato, *Philebus*** (Oxford University Press)
Aristotle, *The Nicomachean Ethics***, trans. J. A. K. Thompson (Penguin Classics)
Epicurus, *Letters and Maxims***, from *Essential Epicurus*, trans. Eugene O'Connor (Prometheus Books)
Epictetus, *The Discourses of Epictetus** (Everyman Series, Phoenix)
Marcus Aurelius, *Meditations**, trans. Maxwell Staniforth (Penguin Classics)
Michel de Montaigne, *The Complete Essays*** (in particular 'On educating children' and vol. III), trans. M. A. Screech (Penguin Classics)
Benedict Spinoza, *Ethics****, trans. G. H. R. Parkinson (Oxford University Press)
Arthur Schopenhauer, *Wisdom of Life and Counsels and Maxims***, trans. T. Bailey Saunders (Prometheus Books), and also *The World as Will and Representation*, trans. E. F. J. Payne (Dover)
Friedrich Nietzsche, *Thus Spake Zarathustra*** (Penguin Classics)
Alain (Émile-Auguste Chartier), *Minerve ou de la sagesse** (Gallimard)
Albert Camus, *The Myth of Sisyphus**, trans. Justin O'Brien (Penguin Books)
Pierre Hadot, *Philosophy as a Way of Life: Spiritual Exercises from Socrates to Foucault***, trans. Michael Chase (Blackwell)
Clément Rosset, *La Force majeure*** (Editions de minuit)
Marcel Conche, *Orientation philosophique*** (Presses universitaires de Frances)
André Comte-Sponville, *Le Mythe d'Icare: Traité du désespoir et de la béatitude** (Presses universitaires de Frances)
Jean-Michel Besnier, *Réflexions sur la sagesse*** (Le Pommier)

Note on extracts

In a number of the translations of extracts from philosophical works, the publishers have found it useful to consult the following texts:

Thomas Kingsmill Aboott (trans.), *Kant's Introduction to Logic*, 1963, Greenwood Press

Aristotle, *Eudemian Ethics*, trans. H. Rackham, 1935, Cambridge, Mass., Harvard University Press

Marcus Aurelius, *Meditations*, trans. Maxwell Staniforth, 1964, Harmondsworth, Penguin Books

Bergson, *The Two Sources of Morality and Religion*, trans. R. Ashley Audra and Cloudesley Brereton, with W. Horsfall Carter, 1935, Greenwood Press

René Descartes, *Discourse on Method and The Meditations*, trans. F. E. Sutcliffe, 1968, Harmondsworth, Penguin Books

Sigmund Freud, 'Mourning and melancholia' in Standard Edition, Vol. xiv: *On the History of the Psycho-analytic Movement; Papers on Metapsychology; and Other Works*. Vol. vi: *The Future of an Illusion; Civilization and Its Discontents; and Other Works*, London, The Hogarth Press and The Institute of Psycho-analysis

Immanuel Kant, 'An answer to the question: What is enlightenment?', in *Practical Philosophy*, trans. Mary J. Gregor, 1996, Cambridge University Press

—, *Critique of the Power of Judgement*, trans. Paul Guyer and Eric Matthews, 2000, Cambridge University Press

—, *Critique of Pure Reason*, preface to 2nd edn, trans. Paul Guyer and Allen W. Wood, 1998, Cambridge University Press

—, *Groundwork for the Metaphysics of Morals*, trans. Arnulf Zweig, 2002, Oxford University Press

—, 'On the impossibility of an ontological proof of god's existence', in *Critique of Pure Reason,* trans. Guyer and Wood

—, *Opus posthumus*, trans. Eckart Förster and Michael Rosen, 1993, Cambridge University Press

G. W. Leibniz, *The Monadology*, trans. Robert Latta, 1898, Oxford University Press

Michel de Montaigne, 'An Apology for Raymond Sebond'; 'On educating children'; 'On experience'; 'On affectionate relationships'; 'On physiognomy'; 'On repenting'; 'On schoolmasters' learning'; 'To philosophize is to learn how to die'; in *The Complete Essays*, trans. M. A. Screech, 1991, Harmondsworth, Allen Lane

Blaise Pascal, 'The Memorial', in *Pensées*, trans. A. J. Krailsheimer, 1966, Harmondsworth, Penguin Books

Plato, *Phaedo*, in *The Works of Plato, Vol. 3*, trans. Thomas Taylor and Floyer Sydenham, 1996, Frome, Prometheus Trust

—, *The Republic*, trans. Desmond Lee, 1974, Harmondsworth, Penguin Books

Jean-Jacques Rousseau, *A Discourse on Inequality*, trans. Maurice Cranston, 1984, Harmondsworth, Penguin Books

—, *The Social Contract*, trans. Maurice Cranston, 1968, Harmondsworth, Penguin Books

Benedict Spinoza, *Ethics*, trans. G. H. R. Parkinson, 2000, Oxford, Blackwell

—, *On the Improvement of Understanding*, trans. R. H. M. Elwes, 1883 (rp 1955), New York, Dover

St Anselm, *The Prayers and Meditations of St Anselm, with the Proslogion*, trans. Benedicta Ward, 1973, Harmondsworth, Penguin Books

St Augustine, *Confessions*, trans. R. S. Pine-Coffin, 1961, Harmondsworth, Penguin Books

Ludwig Wittgenstein, *Notebooks 1914–16*, eds. G. H. von Wright and G. E. M. Anscombe, trans. G. E. M. Anscombe, 1961, Oxford, Blackwell

—, *Tractatus logico-philosophicus*, trans. C. K. Ogden, 1922, London, Routledge and Kegan Paul